Ride a V

An epic 9,000 mile ri   ⌐urope

by

William Holt

The Long Riders' Guild Press

www.thelongridersguild.com

ISBN: 1-59048-044-9

To the Reader:

The editors and publishers of The Long Riders' Guild Press faced significant technical and financial difficulties in bringing this and the other titles in the Equestrian Travel Classics collection to the light of day.

Though the authors represented in this international series envisioned their stories being shared for generations to come, all too often that was not the case. Sadly, many of the books now being published by The Long Riders' Guild Press were discovered gracing the bookshelves of rare book dealers, adorned with princely prices that placed them out of financial reach of the common reader. The remainder were found lying neglected on the scrap heap of history, their once-proud stories forgotten, their once-glorious covers stained by the toil of time and a host of indifferent previous owners.

However The Long Riders' Guild Press passionately believes that this book, and its literary sisters, remain of global interest and importance. We stand committed, therefore, to bringing our readers the best copy of these classics at the most affordable price. The copy which you now hold may have small blemishes originating from the master text.

We apologize in advance for any defects of this nature.

CONTENTS

ILLUSTRATIONS

CHAPTER ONE

Horse and Man Meet

One day in the little town of Todmorden in Yorkshire I saw a white horse. Remembering what superstitious folk told me when I was a boy I spat three times and took a secret wish. Looking a second time I was struck by the darkness of what was behind him. He was hauling an old rag-and-bone cart loaded with old iron. It was incongruous. His white robe was immaculate, his mane valiant, his tail nearly touched the ground. As he approached he looked at me and came to a stop. Whether his driver pulled him up or whether he stopped of his own accord I shall never know. But it was fate. I looked into a pair of sweet eyes. But he was thin. And the vision of his bright eyes was narrowed by a heavy pair of dirty leather blinkers. What on earth was such a heavenly horse doing in such a cart? I spoke to the driver, an elderly, handsome, sun-tanned man with black curly hair now turning grey. In reply to my questions he told me that he had only recently arrived in Todmorden from Leeds. The horse's name was Trigger.

'Where is his stable?'

'He has no stable.'

When I inquired where he put the horse at night the man said that Trigger had always lived in the open air. He was born in the open air. In Todmorden at night he was turned out to graze on the railway embankment. 'Poor thing,' I murmured, but the eyes that were fixed on me were not sad, they were gay. As the enchanting white horse moved away dragging the discordant cart I noticed that Trigger had only one shoe.

I stood for a moment, touched by a strange emotion, a sympathetic yearning which stirred up fanciful ideas. It was

8

much more than a fellow-feeling. It was as if a window had suddenly been opened with a vista into another world. Then like a thunderbolt the decision came. With a wildly beating heart I turned and followed. When the cart stopped again I hurried and caught up and asked the driver if he would sell his horse. Trigger's alert ears were listening and he turned his head and looked at me. And I saw in his eyes that allure.

The driver smiled and shook his head. He looked at me in silence for a while then said that I would have to buy the cart too. He told me that he was not doing very well. He had been thinking of getting rid of the horse. Things were going from bad to worse. He was ill and he wanted to get a job inside.

I offered to buy the whole outfit. 'Come and see me to-morrow,' he said and drove away.

That night I went to look at Trigger on his railway embankment. I stood some distance away on a bridge, hidden from him by the iron plates. He was leisurely cropping the tall weeds and scanty grass, a white ghost in the darkness. He had his back to me. Suddenly an express train thundered under the bridge in steam-smothered light. Trigger's head shot up, he shied and trotted along the steep embankment. Some sparks fell among the weeds. When the last lighted coach had thundered by I could hear his feet crunching in the cinders. He stopped, recovered, then began to rub himself against a telegraph post. After a good rub he shook himself and began to bite at his hairs where the belly-band of his harness had been. For quite a long while after this he stood still with his back to the wind, shifting his weight from one foot to the other, gently lifting one forefoot or the other like fins, his shaggy mane which fell partly on the right side and partly on the left blowing in the wind. There was no animal anywhere near to share his loneliness but he appeared to be content and happy. I did not disturb him.

Next day I bought him, the two-wheeled cart, the old iron and everything. I led him up the hill to my old house

near the moor, dumped the cart and its load and removed
his heavy harness. His cumbersome padded leather collar
had to be turned upside down to get it over his head. He
held his head down and couched his ears to help me to get
it off. When I had got everything off I picked up the heavy
blinkers, held them up before his eyes and with a grand
gesture flung them as far away from him as I could.

He understood.

Around my Elizabethan house I have park land and
pasture and some farm buildings. In the barn Trigger buried
his nose in a bucket of oats, biting deeply and greedily into
them, glancing sideways at me with some surprise. Evidently
he was not used to such wholesome and tasty food. I ruffled
his crooked mane. Obediently he stepped sideways when I
touched his flank, lifting his dainty feet gracefully like a
ballet dancer and placing his back feet neatly close together.
I saw that he had an old-healed scar on the front of his near
stifle. It looked as if at some time he had been impaled. It
had not been stitched. After he had eaten all his oats he took
a sniff at my sleeve.

His surprise at being fed with oats was as nothing to his
astonishment on being turned out loose into one of my fields.
He eyed the stretch of grass and bounded joyously forward,
watched with jealous interest by the two Kilnhurst dogs – a
great Newfoundland and a tiny Shih Tzu. He gave a gay
snort, kicked his hind heels sideways high into the air and
feeling the soft turf under him began to gallop.

All of a sudden he stopped. Standing perfectly still he
lowered his head, sniffed delicately at the grass, his nose only
just touching the tips, the extreme tips. Then he flopped
down sideways and began to roll.

The two dogs barked furiously.

Trigger shot out his forelegs and got up. With his neck
straight out, his back level, his tail sticking out, he looked
oblong. He shook himself so violently that he staggered. After
this salute to freedom he began to graze the succulent grass,
all his graceful curves back again, his tail cascading to the
ground.

That first night, so that he would know without any doubt

that this was now his home, I shut him in the barn with plenty of hay and deep straw. His powerful neigh next morning when he heard my footsteps shook the barn. His deep-chested roar was like that of a wild animal. I opened the door and he looked at me, then he gave vent to a series of high-pitched whinnying squeals – far higher than any human voice could reach – as much as to say: 'Why haven't you come to me before?' This protest was followed at once by a series of deep, joyous belly whinnies, powerful, deep, chuckling belly notes that echoed through the barn like the plucking of the strings of a bass fiddle.

This was in the far-off days of my meeting with Trigger, before I ever thought of riding him, before I ever dreamed of the long journey we were to make together. At first when I met this magic horse and brought him to Kilnhurst I adopted him as one does a stray dog for the pleasure of making him happy, of seeing him eat and sleep and grow well and sturdy in security. I bought him as a pet. I did not realise at that time that it was he who had adopted me. I had rescued him from drudgery and possible slaughter, and he had come to bear me away. This beautiful white Arab horse had come to me not out of misery – he has a happy-go-lucky contented nature – he had come to me out of bondage to a greater happiness, to someone whose tastes and inclination were his own, to someone whose love like his was a love of freedom. And he had brought to me, though I did not realise it at the time, the means of a release from the bondage of humdrum life. It was he who had rescued me.

It was inevitable that I should ride him. He began to follow me about like a dog, everywhere, even down into the town. In his delight in my company when he began to trot I had to run. So I bought a saddle. This was the beginning. He wanted it. He wanted me to run away with him. Never were the longings and wishes of two beings so much akin. Our rides grew longer and farther afield. I was a boy again and we were like two schoolboys who had resolved to play truant – permanently.

At first I had the arrogance to believe that I was showing him a new world of freedom but I soon found that it was he, not I, who was leading the way and showing me a world that I had never seen before. When at last I realised this I often dropped the reins and let him choose the way. He led me to places that I had never seen before – some quite near my home. Quiet spots, secret almost, only a minute's gallop from the busy road, secluded out-of-the-way places that could only be reached on foot or on horseback. There in these hidden spots, sheltered by grassy banks, Trigger and I listened to the whispering trees.

One day Trigger watched me with more than usual curiosity, I was fastening a rolled-up blanket and waterproof ground-sheet to the saddle. And I hung a pair of waterproof canvas saddlebags over his saddle. These rested on each side of him like folded wings. He sniffed at them with great interest. Later they proved to be wings, for both of us. I am not a rich man. Into these bags went some copies of a story I had written called *The Wizard of Whirlaw*. I planned to sell these on our journey to provide the means of our livelihood.

That night after I had let him loose on grass at the edge of a wood Trigger again watched me intently. He saw me turn his saddle upside down for a pillow, unroll my blanket over my ground-sheet, and then, to his astonishment, lie down to sleep. As if he could not believe this really to be true he grazed slowly and thoughtfully, moving round me in smaller and smaller circles, watching me out of the corner of his eye in the growing darkness, his ears turned towards me. Finally he came to a halt and stood over me, his forefeet at the edge of my ground-sheet, his head high, silhouetted among the stars.

In the morning when I awoke he was lying by my side.

Sometimes when talking to farmers and selling my books I would point to the rocks of Whirlaw in the far distance.

Trigger, grazing near me, listened. There were moments like a dream, when the white horse with his saddlebags, his head down grazing, his mane blowing in the wind, seemed to be all mixed up with *The Wizard of Whirlaw*.

One day I rode Trigger up to the foot of the pile of rocks that had inspired my tale. I drew out my hunting horn and blew a long blast. Trigger and I listened to the echo among the rocks.

A weaver in Todmorden spoke to me one day:

'You are lucky to have Trigger.'

'I know.'

'What I mean is that he might have been dead.'

'You mean slaughtered?'

'Well, maybe that, but what I mean is that I once saved his life. I was going to work early one morning soon after he had arrived in Todmorden and Trigger was lying on the ground. He had been tethered to a post on a bit of grass and the short rope had got entangled and was fast round his neck. He was lying nearly strangled. I hadn't a knife with me. I ran back and got the scissors. He was at his last gasp when I cut him loose. I had to help him to get up.'

I looked at Trigger while the weaver was telling me this. His eyes were gay and he wore the same happy-go-lucky expression that had struck me when I first met him pulling the rag-and-bone cart with its load of old iron.

CHAPTER TWO

First Adventures

Kilnhurst, my ancient stone house with walls several feet
thick, was standing at the time of the Field of the Cloth of
Gold, and is mentioned in a deed of bequest dated 1521. It
was a secret meeting place of Catholics in the reign of Henry
VIII. Trigger enjoys the freedom of my land. Outside the
study where I write is a lawn and there Trigger comes and
stands, his back to me, his ears turned to me, listening to
my typewriter. The walls are so thick nothing can be heard
through them but he can hear through the window. If he
hears my typewriting machine stop he looks round and walks
round to the kitchen window where I am making tea. Horses
are quieter where many horses have been before. Like ourselves they sense the peace of very old dwelling-places and
farms. The latest wing of my house, which was added over
two centuries ago to house wool, has an ornamented arched
top doorway which is reached by a flight of stone steps outside. The steps are deeply worn by the tread of feet and so
are the stones which are embedded at the foot where today
there still remains part of the ancient causeway used by
pack-horses in the olden days. Horses have worn the causeway pavement hollow, and bow-shaped tread-worn hollows
in the bottom steps show where the men took a short cut
when going up the steps.

No mechanically propelled vehicle has a right to pass along
my private toll-road which crosses my land. Only cattle and
horses. Even the Royal Mail when it ceased to be horse-
drawn had to be re-routed in accordance with the deeds of
this estate which are written on sheepskin.

By riding Trigger along my private toll-road and down to
the canal bank I can reach the outskirts of Halifax, follow-

ing the tow-path of the disused canal. The level tow-path cuts off miles of hilly road and by-passes the towns of Hebden Bridge, Mytholmroyd, and Luddendenfoot. In some places it is a wilderness of willows, silent save for the noise of falling waters plunging into the depths of old locks. The ground is soft on the tow-path except for the cobbled by-washes where Trigger splashes the water with his feet over the moss-covered stones and drinks. He nibbles the tender reeds between his sips. They are very green and juicy near the water. Sometimes he is startled by pigs galloping across a field or when a water fowl flees from us into the reeds. But he is sure-footed. He walks near the edge of the pavement under the arched bridges so that the saddlebag does not touch the wall.

About ten miles along the Pennine valley from Todmorden the canal passes under the spur of a steep hill. The tow-path goes through what is called the Long Tunnel. Here the water is deep and it is dark.

One afternoon I was riding through this tunnel when a schoolboy ran into the tunnel exit ahead of us. Trigger was walking near the edge to keep the saddlebag clear of the slimy wall. He shied, startled, and we plunged into the canal. In a split second we were both submerged in the cold water.

Trigger began to swim at once, his nostrils just clear of the water, his withers covered, and I, having got out of the saddle swam by his side. We made for the daylight at the end of the tunnel. I was terribly anxious because the water-proof saddlebags were filling with water from the top. Soon they would be like millstones. To undo the buckles and get the saddlebags off in the water with Trigger swimming was difficult if not impossible. We got to the end of the tunnel and Trigger at once tried to climb out on to the bank. He got his forefeet on to the bank but fell back with me under him. He had several tries but the bank was too high. He gave it up and swam to the other side. If there had been a field at the opposite side we could have got out but instead we were faced with a cliff of sheer rocks fifty feet high. We were trapped.

I swam across to Trigger to make an attempt to get his

saddlebags off. He was quicker than I was in finding some means of self-preservation. His neck and shoulders rose out of the water. He had touched bottom and found a sloping narrow ledge. He managed to scramble along the ledge out of the water. I joined him there and at once took off his saddlebags and saddle. He stood perfectly still. He did not even shake himself.

I prayed and thanked God for this ledge. At least Trigger was now safe from drowning. Then I waited for a while thinking that the boy who had seen what had happened would have told somebody. He had run away quickly. There might come some help of some sort. But as time went on I began to fear that the boy might have kept silent about the accident in case he got blamed for it. The canal at this point is a lonely spot. It was no good shouting for help. Nobody would hear. Night was coming on.

After a long wait I swam across the canal to look for a place where Trigger could climb out on to the bank. In a shallow part some distance from the tunnel mouth were reeds but these are very dangerous. A horse could get his feet entangled in the reeds and in his struggle to free himself from the reeds and mud might get drowned. The only place I could find was at the other end of the tunnel where some stones and debris had fallen in. Trigger's heart-rending neigh came to me, echoing through the long tunnel. He thought I had abandoned him. I ran back to comfort him. I swam across and got him to come into the water with me but he refused absolutely to swim into the tunnel. I let him turn back and scramble on to the ledge again.

What could be done now? We were marooned. I caressed his wet mane. Suddenly his head shot up, his ears pricked. A man's head had bobbed up over a wall across the canal. Trigger saw him first. Another head appeared, and then another. There was silence. Nobody spoke. Nobody moved. But someone must have gone for help for presently a police-man's helmet appeared. Head and shoulders over the wall he studied the horse and man on the ledge. Then with great speed and a hubbub of voices the tender of the Sowerby Bridge fire brigade appeared behind the wall. Trigger was watching with intense interest. My deepest feeling now was one of shame to be the cause of this trouble. Helmeted firemen leapt over the wall. What could they do with ladders? They were bringing ladders over the wall. My misgivings increased when they extended ladders, two ladders side by side, across the canal and placed planks on them. Two firemen came across. They carried my saddlebags across and invited me to follow them with the horse. But I was having none of that. If Trigger slipped his foot might get between the planks or the rungs and he might break a leg. It was too risky. At present he was whole and sound. Some other way would have to be found. A barge or a large boat would have been the best solution but the canal was disused. Some of the locks had been unworkable for years.

Looking at the narrow planks an idea occurred to me. Why not make a ramp with them side by side on the other bank? I could then swim Trigger across and he could climb up the ramp. I shouted the suggestion across the canal and it was agreed that this was the best thing to do. But Trigger turned back after swimming a few yards. He preferred the safety of the ledge to the terrifying planks and the shouting firemen who were standing on the planks in the water to prevent them from floating. By this time Trigger was trembling, almost in panic.

A second team arrived with a strong rope net and lengths of stout rope. It was the R.S.P.C.A rescue squad led by Midgely Batty of Halifax. I lifted the net over Trigger's hind quarters and fastened it round his body. Two long ropes now stretched across the canal, fastened at the other end to a tree. I mounted Trigger and urged my frightened horse into the water again. He refused to be led. Once in the water he swam across the canal and there was no turning back this time. Firemen, a policeman, and some of the factory workers were hauling on the ropes. I dismounted and Trigger scrambled up the ramp. Near the top he slipped on his belly with two legs off one side but we managed to roll him on to the bank where he stood up and the net was taken off. There was an air of dignity about the horse now. He shook himself and was silent. Everybody was talking excitedly. A woman had come with tea and she gave me a dry cigarette and lit it for me. I was a woeful sight dripping in my soaked clothes. My blanket which was tightly rolled in my waterproof sheet was not wet through. I threw it over Trigger. A man who lived not far away took charge of my saddlebags while I went with Trigger into Sowerby Bridge to get him a warm bran mash.

Next door to the fire station are some public baths. The superintendent there put my clothes into the huge spin dryer while I had a bath. Trigger meanwhile was happily munching his warm meal in the forecourt. When the superintendent threw my clothes to me they were warm and practically dry. Everybody now expected me to return home but I did not see the point of riding back nearly ten miles in the dark. Trigger had been soaked many a time in the rain and was already nearly dry. Instead we went to a field on the bank of the river Ryburn at Triangle where we had often slept before. My saddlebags were drying out in the boiler-house of Henry Sagar's dye-works. Both of us slept soundly through the night, Trigger lying closer to me than he had ever done before. Danger shared had brought us closer together.

Next morning, apart from the crumpled appearance of my hacking jacket and my linen, I did not appear any worse. Trigger was as fresh as a daisy. He was frisking and snorting to get near Bonnie, a pony he had met before and who lived in a field nearby. Judging from his appearance he had completely forgotten our adventure in the canal. But deep down both of us had learned a lesson which would make us more cautious in the future.

Trigger and I rode deep into the West Riding, sleeping in fields on the hillsides or on the moors, the sky full of stars, the valleys full of lights. How strange the West Riding was now, seen from the saddle and from hills in the middle of the night in full moonlight. Deep thoughts came to me during these rides. I began to think of longer journeys, far, far away.

We slept in the open in all kinds of weather. Now more than ever I was resolved that Trigger was fit to face the hardships of the long journeys I had in mind. Walking by the side of Trigger up steep hills in the Pennines I imagined the two of us ascending the slopes of the Chiltern Hills. It was exciting. My lucky white horse had shown me new places nearer home, I would now love to show him places over the hills and far away. Perhaps one day we might be riding through the Alps! Who could say what adventures were awaiting us?

CHAPTER THREE

Ghosts in Pendle Forest

'You're not a local man?'

The farmer's wife looked at me with curiosity. Her face was thoughtful as she read the sign on my saddlebag painted in yellow fluorescent letters. 'The Wizard of Whirlaw.'

'Oh! You're the man on horseback,' she exclaimed suddenly. She served me with the milk I had asked for.

I was riding towards Whalley. I could see the old Abbey and Whalley church with its old stone coffins in the graveyard. There was no mist over Pendle Hill. A heavy storm was brewing. The sky was almost black. A rumble of distant thunder could be heard as I inquired at an inn for a field where I might sleep that night with my horse. The innkeeper had no field but his sister had married a farmer. 'They are not on the telephone but she is visiting friends in Brierfield who have a telephone.' The thunder came nearer. A few minutes later he gave me this message: 'It's all right. She says you can stay there. You've to go to their farm at the top of Pendle Forest and tell her husband that she has sent you.'

I was not far now from Rough lee, where Alice Nutter once lived, and where Mother Demdyke, Mother Chattox and other Lancashire witches were often seen. We were deep in the Lancashire witch country.

Heavy rain began to fall. At first the forest gave shelter but soon the rain-water was falling from the trees. It was a cloud burst. A sudden mutter of thunder burst into a crash. Between the flashes of lightning the darkness was so intense that I had to rely on my horse to keep to the road.

Suddenly he stopped dead. I dismounted to see what was

19

the matter. Water came up to my knees. We had come to a gate. I opened it and we passed through. The trees were hissing in the rain and a wind sprang up, increasing in fury. There was something malignant about this darkness in summer. Trigger was trembling.

All of a sudden Trigger's head shot up and he snorted.

Two dim specks of light were bobbing about in the eerie darkness. They came nearer. The colour of these mysterious lights was yellowish green like two eyes. I drew my horse aside among the trees and climbed into the saddle in case he bolted. All was silent now save the hissing trees and the gurgling of the flood waters. Trigger's ears were pricked towards the horrible lights which glowed phosphorescent.

A flash of forked lightning lit up the forest and I shivered with horror. A ghostly hearse was passing through the dark forest. What made it more dreadful was the speed at which it was travelling. It was macabre. There was something indecent, obscene, in this headlong speed of a hearse. It jolted and bumped over boulders, rocked and bounced and splashed through the water, increasing its speed and appearing to rise into the air as it disappeared into the darkness.

When I got to the farm it was deserted. No response came to my continuous knocking. I stood for a while sheltering in the doorway of an outhouse wondering what to do. I was still shuddering at the thought of that strange funereal sight in the forest. The door of the outhouse was ajar. My electric torch battery was nearly flat but in its dim ray I could just make out some rusty chains festooned with cobwebs hanging from the ceiling. Some mildewed bags lay among rotting wooden boards. One looked like a corpse that had fallen out of the boards.

Torrential rain was now falling. I took off the saddlebags and put them out of the rain just inside the door and stood in the spine-chilling loneliness of the deserted farm.

Meanwhile a man had arrived at a public house at the edge of the forest, his face as white as a sheet.

'I've seen a ghost.'

'Where?'

'In Pendle Forest.'

He swallowed a glass of brandy at a gulp, then said:

'I saw a man on a horse among the trees. He was wearing a long cape. And on the side of the horse in fiery letters was, "The Wizard of Whirlaw".'

At the other side of the forest while this man was telling of his experience I was waiting in the outbuilding doorway of the lonely farmhouse. It seemed to me that I could hear rustling behind me. Something soft and clammy touched my ear. I cried out 'Ah...!' It might have been a cobweb loosened by the wind but I stepped involuntarily out of the doorway and Trigger shied nervously.

To get away from that loathsome outbuilding I crossed the farmyard and tethered Trigger to the gudgeon of the barn door. Feeling over the arched doors I found a small wicket door which was not fastened. It was level with my chest. I climbed in and found myself on top of hay. It was an empty cowshed. I slid down into a manger. The shed door was bolted on the inside so I let myself out and went to fetch Trigger. Here was shelter for both of us. But Trigger drew back from the door, snorted with fear and refused to go in. I have heard that animals can see things that we cannot see so I felt uneasy. I explored the fences of a neighbouring field and let him loose. Then I returned to the cowshed and fell asleep on the hay.

A frightful noise woke me. It sounded as if an angry old woman was scolding and spluttering with rage in the farmyard. The cowshed door began to rattle violently as if someone was shaking it. I got up and tiptoed to the door. Suddenly I flung it open. Trees and the farmhouse were outlined against the oncoming dawn. Four enormous turkeys were strutting in the yard. Their gabble became shrill as the door opened.

It was useless trying to sleep again. Walking barefoot, as usual in the morning in wet grass so as not to soak my boots, I fetched Trigger out of the field. The rain had stopped. I gave him a feed of oats from my saddlebag and spread out my things to dry.

The farmer appeared as I was trying to polish my wet boots. He was a thin, wiry man with sharp features and an unsmiling face.

'Oh, so you're there,' he remarked. 'I'd gone to fetch mi' wife last night. I didn't know you were comin' till she told me when I got to Brierfield.'

He was looking at my cape which was spread out on a log.

'So it were thee that I saw last neet!' He said this in a low voice as if speaking to himself.

In the daylight I could now see in the background the radiator of a Rolls Royce. The body was black and had large long windows.

'That's an unusual car for a hill farm,' I said in a light-hearted way.

'Aye. It's an old hearse. I bought it cheap. It's handy for me. It's a good engine, an' there's lots o' room inside.'

He said this in a mournful voice and I thought he looked worried about something. Presently the truth came out as he turned his back on me and said ruefully:

'I generally feed mi' hens theer wheer thi' horse is. But I'll feed 'em in t' yard this mornin'.'

CHAPTER FOUR

Logistics for a Long Journey

I have been a soldier and an officer on active service. It was fascinating now to think of 'logistics' in connection with my own private life, but the idea of a ride through Europe had taken complete hold of me. Although my logistics now were for one horse and one man and there was no war, the difficulties of my projected adventure were not small ones. I had no War Office funds to draw on. It would have to be done off my own bat. Climatic conditions would not be severe but a continental winter – as I knew from experience – could be pretty trying. It would mean that Trigger and I would not have to be caught in a rigorous winter in the mountains of the central massif or on the banks of a frozen Rhine. There was equipment to be considered. We could not turn back to re-design it. My heels behind the stirrups had already worn holes in my canvas saddlebags. The first patches of leather had worn through. Now I had sewn in their place large patches of chrome-tanned raw-hide a quarter of an inch thick. My monsoon cape had got me through the English summer – a good test! – and my sheepskin jacket had kept me warm in twelve degrees of frost. Trigger, as far as clothing goes, was not worried by logistics. In spring he shed hairs, in winter he grew them so thick and long that they curled on him. But he would need fodder.

Trigger's boyhood, living always in the open, eating almost anything and constantly in traffic has made him as tough as a mongrel and he has nerves of steel. His fetlocks had lost some of their spring through years of trotting on hard roads hauling a cart but his feet are far better than mine. I am supposed to be lame. If I had taken any notice of doctors at the end of the First World War I should still be wearing an iron support to my left ankle, bushed in my shoe heel and with a leather strap round my leg below the knee, and walking with two sticks. I threw that gadget out of the train window as soon as I was discharged. I did not like it.

I have never been sick. I like that poem by Dryden:

'Better to hunt in fields, for health unbought
Than fee the doctor for a nauseous draught,
The wise, for cure, on exercise depend;
God never made his work, for man to mend.'

In health and feet, Trigger and I have much in common. And we are in no hurry. We have lots of time. And Time always beats Space. In the gay words of Till Eulenspiegel:

'Wer langsam fährt kommt auch zum Ziel.'

Yes, 'he who travels slowly gets there too.'

But although there was no war there were enemies that we would have to face. By the pressure of economic facts the material world would demand its dues. In the olden days a soldier of fortune could live by his sword. I would have to depend on my paint brush, charcoal sticks and pencil. In England I had been able to travel with my pen, but as my books had not been translated I would have to rely abroad on sketching and painting and selling my work. Fortunately pictures are an international language.

In preparation for a very long journey I began to take longer ones in England as a reconnaissance and preliminary canter. The first of these longer journeys was making a bee-line to the coast in order to test climbing. Instead of taking the main road out of Todmorden we began by climbing the mountain of Flowerscar. We slept the first night on Haslingden Moor, the second by Freckleton Marsh and on the second morning I caught sight of Blackpool tower. Trigger's nostrils spread as he sniffed the sea air. It was raining but I drew out my hunting horn and blew a salute to fortune. I had sold books, and by way of a test had sold some pictures.

Trigger's shoes rang out on the hard promenade and he gave a loud neigh – he had seen the horses in the shafts of

the landaus. Then he stopped. As usual I waited for him to
take it all in. Sea to the horizon, miles of golden sand, the
people. It was staggering and for a moment he even forgot
the landau horses. High masts with fluttering bunting, spinning celluloid wind-vanes, balloons. Hooting electric trams,
bells, klaxon horns, showmen's voices. Then, as we descended
the causeway to the beach, squeals of Punch and Judy, trotting donkeys with jingling bells, the shouts of boatmen. He
pawed the soft sand, digging holes, sniffed and grunted at the
stranded star-fish, tasted the sea-shells. I rode him into the
sea. He drew back from each approaching wave and turned,
dizzy, as the broad sheets of foam receded under him. He
tasted the salt water, but he liked the relief of the warm sea
water to his tired feet. To the delight of the watching
children he pawed high and splashed with his foot. He
spotted a jelly fish and tested it with his nose, giving another
of his low, grunting snorts.

I dismounted, took all his harness off and waded in the
sea with him, splashing water all over him with my hands.
He liked that. When we returned to the warm sand he sniffed
at it, flopped down and began to roll. He was dry in a couple
of minutes. I felt in my pocket to buy him some ice-cream
and a chill ran down my body and out of my feet. All my
money had gone...

People were staring at me, it was impossible to hide my
anxiety. Had my pocket been picked? Impossible! I had
not dismounted after the latest sale of a book when I had
given five shillings change for a pound note. That pound note
and all the others had disappeared – perhaps thirty pounds,
the takings of two days. I would have to sell some more books
quickly or neither I nor Trigger would have any lunch. He
had eaten all his oats. I saddled Trigger and we made for the
promenade. All of a sudden I realised what had happened.
I had been putting banknotes into the left pocket of my
riding breeches and small change into the other. In my left
pocket I carried my hunting horn. When I drew it out under
my cape the rim of the copper horn had caught on my roll
of banknotes, had hooked them out and they had blown
away in the wind. Another lesson.

One of my customers for a book was horrified to hear that I slept at night with my horse in fields. 'Aren't you afraid of being robbed?' He was a smartly dressed man who told me that he was a bank manager. I related to him how I had lost all my money that day without being robbed. He was even more horrified. 'Dear me! You should keep your money in a safe place!' He also advised me to bank it each day. 'You can pay it in at any bank.' Then he whispered to me confidentially, 'I always carry with me a five pound note in case of emergency.' He put his lips close to my ear and whispered hoarsely, 'I keep it here' – he tapped his shoe with the end of his neatly rolled umbrella – 'in my sock.'

'Now for some oats,' I said to Trigger when the bank manager had gone. 'We have money in the kitty.' Trigger was pulling me towards the landau horses. They were tossing their nosebags and eyeing Trigger. I spoke to one of the drivers. He was a tall, slim, dark, handsome man with side-whiskers, his hat tilted jauntily on one side. He told me that I could get chop, bran, and oats where he stabled. 'Any time, evening, or early morning. Ask for Johnnie Landau. That's my name.'

This meeting with Johnnie Landau led to some strange adventures behind the scenes in Blackpool for Trigger and me.

The donkeys were returning from the beach. Their dainty feet and jingling bells echoed under the railway viaduct. Trigger and I followed them, past their own stables, and then went on to the stables of the landau horses. Trigger's ears pricked at the sounds of buckets and the munching of hay. The landaus were parked wheel to wheel, shafts upturned. Johnnie Landau was waiting for me with water and fodder for Trigger. He took me into the Malt Shovel inn next door. A cherubic young man five foot high beamed at me. 'Meet John Gilmore, "The Mighty Atom",' said Johnnie. 'Drives a landau in summer, does turns in the theatres and clubs in winter. Married to an ex-circus girl – a trapeze artist. And meet Gilbert Cardwell, veteran winner of the

Landau Cup. Been driving since he was twelve. And Dick Hornby, veteran driver, eighty-two; and Bert Cronshaw, "King of the Cabmen" – used to drive a four-in-hand.' And so the introductions went on.

'Your friend Johnnie Landau has an odd name,' I remarked to Gilmore. 'He has always gone under that name,' was his reply. 'Nobody knows his real name. He was born of gipsy parents.'

Some of the drivers own their own landaus and live in ramshackle huts among the sand dunes, their horses with shaggy fetlocks grazing in a wilderness of tall grasses among old landaus with broken wheels. Trigger and I spent several nights sleeping in the open there among the tall tufts of grasses that bend in the gusts of wind from the sea.

Just as my horse, Trigger, had brought me into touch with the landau men as we travelled about the north of England, he brought me into close touch with farmers, fishermen, weavers, miners, shopkeepers, publicans, nurses, nuns, housewives, people of all classes, rich and poor, children and old folk. Even before I blew my hunting horn children would come running, their bare knees flashing, and they would follow me as if I were the Pied Piper. Outside a school yard one day the schoolmistress had to plead with me to let the children come into the school.

All this was in preparation for the long journey through Europe. At Kilnhurst I designed my kit, fitted myself out, and on my saddlebags I embroidered as my crest the White Rose of York.

CHAPTER FIVE

Riding South

The day of our departure had come at last. I rode down into the town and passed the first milestone: 'Two hundred miles to London.'

We crossed the border from Yorkshire at Summit in the Pennines. The plain of Lancashire spread out before us. What a panorama! Factory chimneys everywhere. At Middleton, looking towards Oldham, there are more mill chimneys in sight than at any other place anywhere in the world. Before entering the densely built-up area of Manchester we slept our first night at the very last farm before the city – Lion Fold Farm.

Next day we crossed the Mersey at Stockport and began to leave the industrial region behind. Hedgerows appeared. The houses of Cheshire had brighter colours. The rain ceased. I dismounted to roll up my cape. Some schoolgirls were coming out of a school. I overheard one of the girls say:

'Oh! I'd give anything, *anything!* (she stamped her foot) 'to have a horse like this.'

Riding on the grass verges my saddlebags brushed the hedgerows. I snatched at the elderberries and crushed some of them in my mouth. Trigger had a go when he saw me do it but he did not like them. Passing motorists waved to us. Some stopped and I sold a book or two, others looked as if they wanted to stop but the speed bug had bitten them and after slowing down and smiling they went on. Poor devils, I thought. Shut in. From time to time Trigger gave a low grunting snort which sounded like a purr or a snore – 'Hurrrrrh' – and I knew that he was happy. And I answered back in his horse language, 'Hurrrrh!'

At Adlington in the afternoon a man came out of a gate into the middle of the road. 'I've got a little farm,' he said. 'Bring your horse in. I'll give him a feed and you can stay here for the night.' I looked at the sky. I had planned to get farther before dark but a big dark cloud heralded more rain so I turned in and we stopped for the night at Hope Green Farm.

Crossing the river Bollin next morning we rode into the silk manufacturing town of Macclesfield. The fishmonger in the main street rushed out of his shop like a boy and wanted to buy a book. He refused to accept the five shillings change for a pound. 'Buy Trigger some carrots,' he said. Girls tapped on the window panes of the silk mills and threw kisses. Girls in the street crowded round Trigger, patting him. 'Ay! Aren't you a softy! What lovely long eyelashes you've got. And look at his wavy tail!' There were lip-stick marks on Trigger's white neck as we rode out of Macclesfield.

Mist came with the darkness. I turned my horse into a field at Boarded Barn Smithy near Scholar Green and went for a meal at The Bleeding Wolf. I could not find Trigger in the thick fog when I returned. He came up behind me and touched me with his nose. But during the night the fog cleared and the stars were brilliant.

Off early to Newcastle under Lyme I saw what appeared to be a false dawn. The ghostly blue light proved to be a hill with arc lamps, and what a long hill! We rested half-way up and I cleaned my boots under an arc lamp. At the junction with the road from Knutsford I had hoped to find a transport café but was disappointed. When a man has slept in a field and has ridden a long way on horseback he can smell bacon and eggs a mile away. Soon I knew. It came into sight. Outlined against the café lights heavy lorries were parked like a herd of giant cattle. Drivers came out to feed Trigger with bread. They reported thick fog farther along the road. Daylight was coming. Mist rested in straight bars in the hollows, the trees rising out of it. Trigger's neck was warm under his mane and the smell of him was sweet, fragrant like hay.

It was after eight o'clock when we first caught sight of a

silvery sun. Trigger's hoofs were now covered with the chocolate-coloured earth of Staffordshire.

Great roadworks stretched ahead, the earth turned up by bulldozers, downhill as far as I could see. On a distant hill the sun lit up an endless conglomeration of new red brick houses. Behind them smoke was rising from the potteries of Stoke on Trent.

How different from the tree-shaded roads of Cheshire with clusters of elderberries weighing down. From the saddle instead of looking into cottage gardens ablaze with dahlias I was now looking over cement mixers at piles of ballast. Trigger's ears were tuning-in but instead of the cawing of rooks and the soft hammering on red-hot iron on an anvil near a village green he could now hear only the staccato din of pneumatic picks and the snarling of heavy gears on gradients. Enormous eight-wheelers with trailers, towering vans, double-decker buses, dwarfed Trigger as they loomed past almost shaving our saddlebags. Many roads were converging from Derby, Nantwich, Burton upon Trent, Stafford, Wellington, and Market Drayton.

I walked for a few miles when we got to the river Trent and then stopped and sat down to look at the map, while Trigger gathered mouthfuls of flowering clover. An old farmer looked at me through his steel-rimmed spectacles:
'So you're travellin' the country, eh? Like John Wesley.'

It was Saturday. Market stalls lined the streets of Stone. Trigger loves celery. A greengrocer was chopping bunches and soon Trigger was crunching a heap of juicy outside sticks while I went to buy a fruit malt loaf and some cheese. 'Is that your horse?' a woman asked when I returned. 'He looked hungry. I nearly turned back and bought him a tea-cake. But I thought his owner might be offended. I love animals. I've never had a horse. Only a dog and cat, but I don't like to see them hungry. Bless him! Take care of him. My bus is comin' . . .'

Another woman came hurrying from a side street and made

for a small boy who had been following us everywhere:
'Stephen! *Stephen!* What are you doing? You haven't
had your breakfast.'

'I don't want mi breakfast on Sat'day,' shouted Stephen,
ducking away from her.

An old man patting Trigger and talking about a horse he
once had said to me, 'I used to put oil of aniseed on my
sleeve. He'd always come to me then.' 'Trigger'll come to me
without that,' I said.

When an old bargee talked to me at Little Stoke where the
river Trent and the canal come close to the road I related
to him our adventure when Trigger fell into the canal in the
Long Tunnel.

'I once had a horse in,' he said. 'Stuck in the reeds, dying
on his back.

'We got him out. Two planks. We rolled him to safety.

'We had to use a pay rope.'

'What's that?'

'A towing rope with a hook.'

The sun was setting as we rode towards Wolverhampton,
Trigger trotting along a high grassy bank. A car drew up
and a man and a woman got out. They invited me to their
home in Wolverhampton. 'You can have a bed, a bath, breakfast...' It was embarrassing. People who don't ride horses
don't understand. They did not say where Trigger could
sleep. And Wolverhampton was ten miles away. A mile is a
mile for a horse. I did not want them to be embarrassed too
so I made some excuse.

The fog was thickening, I dismounted to see if I still had
my electric torch. Then suddenly I remembered the malt
loaf. Where was it? It had disappeared. I was hungry. I felt
sure that I had bought it that day. What happened to it? I
looked at Trigger. He was standing and looking ahead in
innocence, and I knew that he had eaten it. I had left the
saddlebag unbuckled when selling a book in Stafford. When
my back had been turned he had fished deep down for it
with that cunning, prodding, insinuating, contorting upper

lip of his which he can use like a hand or like an elephant's trunk to get into pockets or shopping bags. Yes, the culprit had eaten my fruit malt loaf, swallowed the cellophane wrapping and all.

'Now then, we're going into a field and it's Sunday tomorrow. You've got your oats. What about me?'

No answer.

The fog was now thick. I did not know where we were. According to the map we were near the bank of the river Penk and the Staffordshire and Worcestershire canal, and should be somewhere near Penkridge, but I could not see the canal and we had not crossed a bridge. I walked by the side of Trigger on the right of the road with my torch facing the creeping traffic as darkness fell. It was very dangerous now, we would have to get off the road – my horse is almost the same colour as the fog – but where could we go? A car bent or smashed in a crash can be straightened out but a horse can be maimed or killed outright. I was walking slowly and cautiously feeling with my foot along the edge of the road, walking Trigger on the grass, but another danger faced us. Not being able to see more than a yard or two ahead in the fog and darkness it was impossible to know whether I had come to a fork. Indeed I was afraid that I had already got off the main road. For some time now no cars had passed.

We came to a spot where the narrow grass verge stopped. A road led off to the right. Was it a side road that we had to cross or a sharp bend of the main road? I dared not lead Trigger out across an unknown road so I tethered him to the trunk of a hawthorn bush while I walked across in the fog to explore. I felt with my hands outstretched and came to a wall, a smooth wall with a rounded top. Was this the bridge? I groped for a stone and threw it over the wall. I heard a splash. It was the bridge on the map. With hands outstretched I went back to join Trigger. For a moment my heart almost stopped beating. He was not there. Fearing that he had got loose I blew a low note on my hunting horn. An answering whinny came from quite near. He was still tethered.

We crossed the bridge and just beyond my hand felt some

Photo: The Guardian

Above I dreamt of journeys over the hills and far away. *Below* We slept on the grass like two schoolboys playing truant.

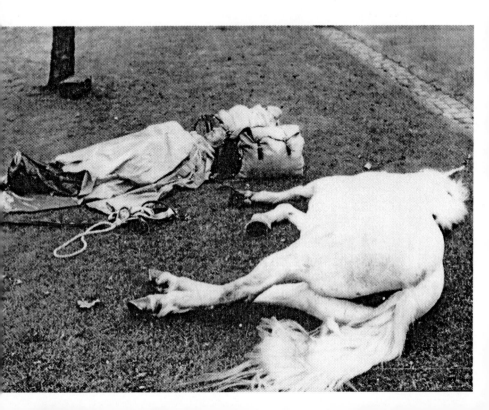

Southward bound. All Europe before us. Good-bye to Flo and Toya.

A drop of ale in Trigger's oats. When having a drink I hate to leave my best friend outside. But Trigger prefers it that way, even in snow.

Photo: C. Kent & Son

wooden railings and a cottage gate. A few yards away was a rime-framed lit-up window. The man who came to the door said that there was a farm, 'just over the bridge and turn right.' Trigger was soon in safety in a field.

Fearing that we might be fog-bound and seeing that it was Sunday next day I decided to ride on to Wolverhampton on the footpath at the side of the dual carriageway in the very early hours when no one was about.

It was a strange eerie ride. The headlights of lorries coming from behind threw an enormous trembling shadow of a gigantic horse and rider on to the curtain of fog ahead. This made Trigger shy. When at last sodium vapour lamps cut through the fog and lit up the pavement with a cold glare the streets of the suburbs of Wolverhampton were deserted. It was like empty stage scenery. Then a party of revellers appeared. They looked like actors in the unnatural light. Mounted on my horse I must have looked strange to them. They were returning from an all-night ball and they laughed with derision when I asked if a café was open anywhere.

Their voices died away and the clip-clop of Trigger's feet echoed through the empty streets of Wolverhampton. Daylight came at the top of a hill. Trigger began to graze. The houses in the suburb showed no sign of life so I took off his harness and lay down on my ground-sheet and folded blanket.

When I awoke it was late, the world was astir, the sun was warm and church bells were pealing. Women were peering out of their windows at this man and horse on the grass verge; some had come out and were standing at their gates, their dogs sniffing and looking at Trigger. I got up and the dogs began to bark. When Trigger got up and shook himself the barking grew shrill.

Trigger, now rested and refreshed, yawned, his jaws wide apart, his lips curling backwards, his two rows of teeth like pincers, Picasso-like. He stretched one back leg out and let it come slowly down. The barking of the dogs left him utterly indifferent. The Sunday morning journey began through a

heavily industrialised area. Men were washing their cars,
tinkering with motor cycles, rooting about in their gardens,
Sunday papers were being delivered, Sunday joints were
roasting. Towns were so close together it was impossible to
see where one ended and another began – Bilston, Coseley,
Tipton, Dudley, Oldbury. I felt hot and uncomfortable in
a world dusty and dry. Less and less grass, more and more
houses. Cafés and shops were closed, the public houses were
not yet open but men were hanging about waiting. Poor
Trigger! Not a blade of grass at all now. I made inquiries
but nobody knew where fodder for a horse could be bought.
I begged a bucket of water in a public house where dogs
sniffed closely at my boots and riding breeches, scenting the
horse, trodden grass and herbs. By a fountain in the city
centre I gave Trigger the remainder of his oats and birds
waited for the scattered grain. Then we went through miles
of dreary streets. It took all the rest of the day to get through
the city of Birmingham. Trigger became very hungry again.
We were in a working-class district. Children began to run
towards Trigger:

'Is it yours?'

'What's its name?'

'What's its second name?'

'How old is it?'

'Only twelve? Oo what a big one. It looks a hundred to
me.'

'It's eatin' an iron thing.'

'Mister! Have you had it since it was a baby?'

The children followed in a crowd along the footpath and
were joined by others, showering me with questions:

'Are you going to milk it?'

'How far have you been?'

'I've been thirty miles,' said one little girl when I told them.

'I've been thirty-ten,' said a much smaller girl.

'Grr! There isn't a thirty-ten,' said a big girl.

Under an arc lamp farther up the hill Trigger spotted
some grass and made for it. It was not very clean and there
was litter on it but I waited for him, and the questions began again:

'Does he eat bread?'

There was a scamper to the houses when I nodded. Along-side the grass were blocks of flats and on the other side of the road were streets of poorer houses. After the older children had run for bread, some very tiny ones asked questions:

'Is that a horse?'

'I wish I 'ad a norse.'

'I have a norse,' said another boy.

'Where is it?' I asked.

'Oh, in the toy box somewhere.'

The boy studied Trigger:

'Are you goin' to sit on it?'

'If you 'ad a cart behind it would you let me 'ave a ride?'

The children were returning at great speed with the bread. While the bigger girls were feeding bread to Trigger, running away and screaming if he stepped towards them, I listened to the innocent comments of the children. One big girl returned for the third time with bread, this time with a loaf. 'Where have you got it?' I asked. 'Sh! I've stolen it,' she whispered. I put Trigger's bit in and moved on. 'Don't give him any more,' I said.

Where were we going to sleep that night I wondered. I looked at my map with my electric torch. We were in Yardley. It was now quite dark and we were surrounded by streets of houses. Trigger was straining to move on. He wanted to get out into the country and I did not blame him.

'Ah, what's this?' Pitch darkness ahead. We had come to the last lamp. Raw cold darkness, like looking into an abyss, and it was past midnight. Some clean fresh grass was on the roadside now. Trigger was the first to use his wits. While I ruminated, Trigger grazed. It was too late to search for a farm. A thin mist hung over the road. It might turn to fog. What better place to sleep than here under the arc lamp? But Trigger would have to be tethered. What could I tether him to? I looked around and found what I needed. Only a few yards ahead was a big oblong metal sign sup-ported by tubular steel posts and on it: WARWICKSHIRE.

CHAPTER SIX

The Midlands

Trigger was flat out asleep on the grass when I awoke. The air was raw. The powerful arc lamp made the road ahead look darker but I decided to push on at once and rest during the day. As soon as I moved, Trigger shot out his forelegs, gathered his hind legs under him and stood up. The saddle-bags were already in place and strapped on when a police car drew up.

'Are you all right?'

'Yes, thank you. What makes you ask?'

'Well when we passed here an hour ago we couldn't believe our eyes – a man and a horse fast asleep on the roadside, and snoring.' The sergeant chuckled. I explained to him why we had stopped at the last lamp.

'We know who you are. We've heard all about you. How far will you get today?'

'Coventry. And a bit farther on.'

'Well good luck to you!'

'What time is it?'

'Half-past four.'

The Z car purred away into the mist.

A few steps in wet grass is enough to soak boots. At the entrance to the airfield near Elmdon I was able to stand off the road on asphalt while Trigger breakfasted on grass. A few miles farther on we turned off the main road and crossed the river Blythe to Meriden. On the village green stands a post with a sign which says: 'This is the middle of England.' Trigger began to graze as much as to say, 'Yes I know all about it. And very good grass this is in the middle of England.' I tethered him to the middle of England while I dragged my sponge in the dew and sponged my face. In the warm morning sun I had begun to nod. A new hazard was the danger of falling asleep in the saddle. And I was looking for a place where I could change my linen before riding into Coventry. A mile or so farther along the road I found an ideal spot. In driving the M.I. motorway a small triangular piece of field had been left. It was fenced, had a gate, and was sheltered on one side by a high hedge. I could take off my sodden boots and Trigger and I could have a well-needed sleep.

A couple of hours later, refreshed and in fine shape, horse and man emerged on to the road without a speck of mud on them. Trigger was brushed, my linen changed, and I had even managed to get quite a shine on my boots. While I was fastening the gate Trigger set off towards Coventry. 'Whoa!' I shouted, running after him. He broke into a trot and spotting a convenient side lane instinctively rejected Coventry. The lane was narrow and muddy. 'Dammit!' I swore. Trigger began to canter. He splashed through the water and the mud which was now well up to our knees. The lane got muddier. Beyond that even Trigger hesitated and I overtook him. The saddle and bags were splashed, as for Trigger himself . . . well, despite my chagrin I had to laugh. The mud would have to dry before I could do anything about it.

No blinds were drawn or shutters closed as we rode through the streets of Coventry covered with mud. I bought oats straight away and gave them to Trigger at once and a crowd gathered round. A Peeping Tom of a policeman pushed his helmet back and scratched the strap under his chin but Trigger munched his oats unconcernedly.

After Birmingham we had been travelling east; from Coventry we turned south-west towards Kenilworth. It was growing dark as we ascended the hill bordered with woodland and bracken. I dropped the reins and let Trigger look for a place where we could halt for the night. He turned into a side lane through the dense wood and we came to a farm called Cryfield Park Grange where the farmer, George Haigh, had just what we wanted – a nice dry field, fenced and with a closed gate. In the field were cattle which Trigger ignored with disdain; the cows, however, were not so aloof. Curious about the strange visitors they came breathing around me, interested in my saddlebags and sniffing as I made my bed. While I was looking at Trigger, one of them got her teeth into my ground-sheet and made off with it. I had to run after it across the field.

It was a wonderful starry night, the air delicious to breathe, so pure and cold. I was snug in my blanket and Trigger was warm by my side. Several times I awoke and was surprised by the brilliance of the stars. A few hours breathing such air in sleep is worth a whole night in a bedroom. Lying on my back I could see the whole of the sky. When Cassiopeia had passed the zenith and the Great Bear had passed the lowest point of the circle and begun to climb, I saddled Trigger. It was four o'clock.

Orion hung glittering in the sky before us. I felt so gay when we reached Kenilworth that I drew out my hunting horn for a lark. Thinking of John Peel I said to myself, 'I'll bring them from their beds,' and as we clattered through the deserted streets I blew a series of merry notes and a long loud blast. Bedroom windows lit up but I had not counted on 'the cry of the hounds'. A man came running across the road when we stopped at a broad grass verge at the other end of Kenilworth:

'I thought the meet was at eight o'clock?'

'What meet?'

'The North Warwickshire Hounds.'

'Where are they meeting?' I was horrified at what I had done.

'Here on this grass.'

'Good God! Who is the master? I must go to him and apologize.'

'Lord Leigh.'

'Where does he live?'

'Here. Thickthorn.' The man pointed to some handsome gates across the road. He told me that he himself used to be a joint-master. His name was Bates, Tom Bates, but he had had to resign as he was suffering from thrombosis.

Lord Leigh accepted my apologies in good humour. He was hurrying to get ready, puzzled on hearing a hunting horn. 'Where have you come from?' he asked. When I had told him that I had slept in a field at Cryfield Park Grange he said, 'What? You must be feeling cold. Would you care for a glass of rum? We shall be moving into Thickthorn cover soon, would you like to join the hunt?'

Dumping my saddlebags and leaving them with Tom Bates I rode Trigger to the meet. All three joint-masters, Lord Leigh, Captain Cartwright and David Dare now understood about my horn – a Yorkshire horn. Trigger was twitching under the saddle watching the hunters and the pack of hounds. The cracking of whips and the notes of another horn excited him. He snorted and thoroughly enjoyed himself.

I was able to stay only about an hour. On the road to Warwick I was telephoning from an hotel when the head waiter tapped on the glass panel:

'Your horse has bolted.'

'How? He's tethered.'

'He's gone.'

Trigger's bridle was lying on the ground. He had pulled the tongues of the buckles through (I was not using a head-stall) and had galloped off to rejoin the hunt.

It was a strange sight, not likely to be forgotten, a riderless horse with saddlebags galloping and jumping without bridle. I dreaded that he might dash through a narrow gap and tear off his saddlebags. He was headed off, rounded up, and came cantering back down the road to the hotel, jumping over the rockery. He was caught by bait. A waitress came out with a bowl of scraps and I was able to throw the bridle and reins over his neck. It was all over. He was obedient now. He had had his fling.

The road out of Warwick to Banbury runs along a low ridge. There is no water. I wonder how travellers managed in the olden days. Many horses must have passed that way. At one point the road crosses the Fosse Way – the old Roman road from Lincoln to Exeter. The day was dry and hot. Trigger was very thirsty. Very few drinking troughs are to be found on roads anywhere today but usually I am able to beg a bucket of water from a cottage. On this road are no cottages, no houses. The farms are far back away from the road in hollows where there is water. There are no rivers, no canals, no streams, no wells. 'To Banbury' the road sign had said at Warwick but it was a long way to Banbury Cross, twenty miles or so, and the road was hard. We were looking hopefully ahead at each bend. How different from the wilderness of Birmingham with houses everywhere. There he had water but no food. Now he had food but no water. At long last we caught sight of a farm and Trigger made for it. Not a soul was there but we found a water tap with a galvanised tin bath under it. We both drank deeply. Our troubles were over. Another bend in the road brought an inn into view. The Gaydon Inn.

'I'm right glad to see you,' said the landlord. 'Would you like something to eat?'

What an understatement! 'Something to eat.' The meal he set before me in a private room with a fire was magnificent – a big pot of tea, bacon and eggs, cold ham with pickles, salad, cheese, cottage bread and fresh farm butter. 'We'll leave you to it,' he said, drawing the curtain as the late afternoon sun was blazing through the window. 'Help yourself. There's plenty more.'

Before I had finished my meal I drew the curtains back and looked out. Behind the inn was a little field. That was where Trigger and I slept that night.

In the morning a powerful wind roared through the tall trees. The landlord and his wife saw us off and waved their hands as Trigger trotted along the level road towards London. The eddying fallen leaves and the ripples on the pools caused by the gusts of wind made Trigger shy. He was in high spirits, giving his little snorts, 'Hurrrrh!' I read the old signposts placed at a height for a man on horseback. What lovely names of villages! – Burton Dasset, Avon Dasset, Knightcote, Fenny Compton . . .

A small crowd was waiting at Banbury Cross including a

man with a cine-camera. A policeman who had seen me on
the road had telephoned to say that I was coming. The
cameraman wanted to take not only a picture of Trigger,
he wanted a lady on the white horse and there she was at
Banbury Cross, waiting – a very pretty pupil from a local
dancing school. But she did not have rings on her fingers
and bells on her toes, which was a pity.

Trigger was quietly grazing on the side of the Oxford
Road in the early evening when a lady came across the road
from a detached house where she had been watching the
horse from her window. She had greying hair and a stately
bearing. She might have been a retired schoolmistress. She
spoke with cultured accent and without smiling:
'Where are you going to stay tonight?'
'In a field somewhere farther along the road.'
'I have a field.'
'Where?'
'Across the road.'
I looked at her house with its garden full of flowers. A
sanded drive ran up the side to a wide gate. 'It's rather early
yet, perhaps I'd better get a few miles farther along the road
to Oxford before stopping,' I said. 'Thank you all the same.'
'It's a nice field . . . Plenty of grass. Good grass.'
'It might rain tonight. Perhaps I'd better be where there
are some big trees.'
'There's a hut in the field. It's clean. There is nothing in
it. You could put your horse in.'
'Oh, Trigger would much rather be outside.' I laughed.
The lady went on to praise the field so much that I felt I
would like to have a look at this wonderful field.
Hatless, with silver hair, the quiet-spoken lady led me and
Trigger across the road and up the immaculate sanded drive.
The field proved to be even more lovely and tempting
than the picture her words had painted. It was like a field in
a fairy tale, full of deep green grass and bright with daisies
and buttercups. Trigger strained over the gate looking at it.
The gate opened with a click and we walked through. The

wooden hut had no floor. Inside it was sweet grass and the front of the hut was open to the south. It was all like a dream, it seemed too good to be true.

The silver-haired lady watched from the gate. I smiled and said, 'I think I'd like to stay here.'

She turned towards her house. I wondered who she was. I called to her, hurrying towards the gate, 'I say! Just a moment...' She stopped to listen with her back to me without turning her head. She listened to my question with her head bent slightly forward and answered it without hesitation as she walked away: 'May I ask... to whom am I indebted for this very kind hospitality?'

'To your horse'.

CHAPTER SEVEN

London

Trigger's shoes were wearing thin by the time I caught sight
of the spires of Oxford. From the saddle I surveyed the
handsome skyline of the university city, pinnacles and domes
cupped on the horizon by trees. Great white clouds sailing
on the west wind dwarfed the low skyline. A university city
dwarfed. As I was riding into Oxford a voice hailed me from
a passing saloon car: 'Hello, Bill!' It was a man from my
home town. He had left Yorkshire that morning and would
be in London before night. How small is the world, in
a car.

'When will you be in London, Bill?'

'Monday.'

It was Thursday.

How big is the world, on horseback. But I was not in a
hurry. I turned from St Giles into quiet Broad Street and
gave Trigger his oats near the gates of Trinity College.
Trigger's arrival had brought out some dons from
Balliol. They bought copies of my book and were amused
when they saw my hunting horn. One of them seemed to me
to be struggling to adjust himself to the idea of an author
in Broad Street riding with his own books. He was nervous,
rather like a shy little boy. When I blew a blast for him with
my horn he laughed with a strange mixture of delight and
derision.

There was no farrier in the city. The nearest was at Thame
twelve miles away and not on the direct road to London
but that did not matter much. I could go on through Princes
Risborough. It began to rain heavily as I rode up the hill
from Magdalen Bridge towards Headington. The farrier at
Thame put all his other work on one side to shoe Trigger.

He examined the Yorkshire shoes with interest. 'We put fewer nails in here,' he said.

I slept with Trigger in a field at Thame, a big field surrounded by a high hedge and a ditch. When I got up, Trigger had disappeared. I set off to look for him in my bare feet. He was not in the field, he was nowhere to be seen. I blew my horn but no answering neigh came. Anxious now, I shouted, 'Trigger! Trigger!' No answer. I climbed a tree so that I could see over the high hedge across the flat countryside but there was no sign of him. Trigger had completely disappeared, lost in Oxfordshire. I blew another loud blast and with a sinking heart heard the sound of my horn die away. In the near distance were the beginnings of streets, houses, back gardens of houses in a row. Beyond them other houses, streets, population, vastness... It had seemed a big world with Trigger. In my mind now loomed an even bigger world. And empty... without Trigger. I am not ashamed to say that I was in tears.

In my bare feet in the long grass I examined every inch of the ditch for hoof prints, my riding breeches in the wet grass were soaked, my feet stung by nettles. If Trigger had got on to the main road I shuddered to think of the hurtling lorries. I put on my boots, covered up my saddle and saddlebags, picked up the bridle and went out of the gate into the road. My intention at first was to report my loss to the police, but as I was fastening the gate I remembered that the night before at that very spot I had heard a distant neigh, perhaps half a mile away, and Trigger had answered. I set off at once in that direction. Every gap in a hedge against the sky now looked like Trigger. I had followed the narrow road round several bends when I caught sight of a white speck perfectly still. At that distance I could not make out whether it was a cow or a horse. I said to myself, it *must* be Trigger. Squeezing myself through a barbed wire fence, crossing fields, climbing over fences, I tore my hacking jacket, my wrists and face were scratched by thorns but I did not care. Yes, it was Trigger, and another horse with him, a black one. Trigger had spotted me but did not move until I came up to him. He let me fondle his wet mane but as soon as I lifted the bridle he bolted, followed by the black mare. He had been rubbing himself on a dirty wet tree and was piebald with large dirty patches on his neck, flank and buttocks. Presently a man appeared at the far end of the field rattling the handle of a bucket and calling, 'Betty! Betty!' The black mare trotted to him and Trigger followed. At the gate I cornered my runaway horse and got the bridle on. The farmer told me how I could get back to my saddlebags by road.

Without stopping to groom him I rode Trigger over the border into Buckinghamshire. Outside an inn at Princes Risborough, tethered to a ring, Trigger had to submit to a thorough scrubbing before he got his oats. After the heavy rain the sun had come out and a fresh breeze was driving great white clouds high over the thick beech woods. In Staffordshire the earth was chocolate-coloured. Trigger's hoofs now looked as if he had been treading in chocolate cream. We were in the chalky country of the Chiltern Hills. What quaint names of the villages: Longwick, Owlswick, Kiblewick, Little Kimble.

At High Wycombe we joined the main road. It was Saturday afternoon, the road packed with cars, the corn-mill closed. I had forgotten the day of the week but I found out where the miller lived and soon Trigger had his nose deep in a mixture of oats and bran and his eyes on the reserve stock I was loading and fastening to the front of the saddle.

Our way now was close to the river Wye in marshy country. Cold rain was falling and judging from the sky there was plenty more to come. We passed through a place very appropriately called 'Loudwater'.

It was dark when we reached Beaconsfield; under the dripping trees, the road lights were reflected dismally in the puddles and on the wet surface of the road. Big, aloof houses in gardens lined each side. What hope here of finding a farm? Not a field in sight. But again, Trigger found the way for me. He crossed the road to a gate. I could see nothing beyond the gate but a big house like the others but I could now smell farmyard manure. No answer came to my knock. I walked round and found windows lit at the back and I was in a wide yard. We had arrived at Wilton Farm. I led Trigger across the yard to a lighted doorway where I could hear the lowing of cattle. A young man called Jack Harding was preparing to milk. He welcomed us and showed me where we could shelter and I took off my dripping cape and shook my wet hat. While sorting out my things I found that someone had pushed into one of my saddlebags a piece of cardboard on which was written, 'Good luck! Someone different.'

We had certainly had good luck in finding a farm late on a Saturday night in a built-up area in pouring rain. In the morning Jack brought a tray of tea and toast for me before milking. The rain had stopped, Trigger was dry, my cape nearly dry. Within half an hour we were at Gerrards Cross and I was thrilled to see London buses and stations of the Underground. Northolt, Greenford and Perivale were soon left behind. We were now on what seemed to be an endless carriageway, broad, smooth, straight, and monotonous on horseback. As the day wore on I began to weary. Trigger was tired too, and hungry. Many cafés were shut. It was Sunday, the worst possible day to ride into London. Lights were going up along the Western Avenue. I began to turn over in my mind the problem of where we were going to sleep. Rain began to fall. We were near White City. Just at the junction of Western Avenue and Wood Lane I saw a café lit up. A cup of tea! And a bucket of water for Trigger.

The proprietor of the café had not the faintest idea of where we could stable. It was like asking for the moon. I was the first horseman who had ever stopped at his café. It was quite dark when I came out. Mounting wearily I rode down Wood Lane towards Shepherd's Bush. It was not so much the distance we had travelled that day, it was the inhospitality of the streets that made both man and horse weary. On my long journeys I had always exulted at the comforting thought that the force of gravity and the resistance of matter made it always possible on earth to lie down anywhere and rest – a great blessing forgotten by all of us except astronauts – and I could lie down and sleep just anywhere. I cast my eyes right and left for some place where we could get off the road and lie down. But the earth was now not only covered with concrete, the space on it was taken up by roads, streets, traffic, buildings. This concrete-lidded, traffic-jammed, poison-fuming world stretched for miles now in every direction. In the drizzling rain of that Sunday night it seemed to me, mounted on my horse, like the end of the world, the very threshold of Hell. I looked round to see if three other Horsemen were following me!

Like a vision in a Dantesque dream a wide gateway appeared. There were lights around it. I drew rein, turned Trigger and rode through. It was apparent by its structure and the notice boards that it was crown property, a military place, probably a barracks. But no sentry stood guard. I rode into the dark square. There was nobody in the lodge. A few windows were lit in the upper storey of a high building. With my monocle in I could just read in the dimness a large sign bearing the crest of the Royal Marines.

'Hello! Hello!' I shouted. There was no response.

I rode around the square in the drizzling rain and then shouted again, and this time, having seen the crest of the Royal Marines, it was 'Ahoy! Ahoy!' I shouted, and still there was no response. I blew my hunting horn and a woman's head bobbed out of a window of an upper storey:

'What do you want?'

'I have a horse. We are tired. We want shelter for the night. We can lie down and sleep anywhere so long as we are off the road.' The woman considered this:

'The caretaker isn't in.'

'Isn't there anybody else?'

'No. I'm all alone. The place is empty now.'

A double line of trees extended along one side of the square. Between them was gravel but at the foot of each tree some grass had grown. 'We'd be all right under one of those trees,' I said. The woman pondered again. Presently she said, 'There's a hut over there. It has been on fire. It's not ours. You could go in there.' The woman then warned me that the entrance gate would be closed at eleven o'clock until seven next morning.

I examined the hut. Half of it had been burned down but what was left would house a dozen horses. Debris blocked the entrance and the floor was two feet above the ground level. I used a door for a ramp but Trigger's eyes dilated and he snorted with fear at the dark silhouette of the hut and the smell of wet charred wood. He refused absolutely to go in. 'Very well. You stay outside then,' I said, rather irritated. But when I had put my saddle and bags under cover I felt sorry for poor Trigger. We had slept together all the way to London. I carried my things out of the hut again and joined him on a patch of grass under a tree. There was just room for Trigger and me. I was falling asleep when I felt Trigger lie down beside me. His shoulders were warm against me. Slowly his head sank down and with a sigh of contentment he let it fall on my knees.

Ought I to go to sleep with a horse's head on my knees? It weighed about twenty-eight pounds. I fondled his mane. He had turned on his side and had stretched his legs out for the night. He snuggled his head into a comfortable position on my knees. What ought I to do? ...

Nature answered my question. I fell asleep.

CHAPTER EIGHT

With the Queen's Horses

I awoke first. Trigger's head was still on my knees. The non-stop day and night London traffic had not disturbed our deep sleep. The rain had stopped but big drops fell with a plop on my waterproof cape. Careful not to move or make a sound I lay thinking of the things I would have to do that day.

Trigger's head bobbed up, his ears pricked. He had heard footsteps on the gravel. The gate was now open. We got up and slipped through the gate unseen into Wood Lane. Buses, lorries, vans, electric trains were moving and in the background were sounds of a monstrous stirring everywhere. The great city was like a sprawling giant waking up after a disturbed night with a hangover. Oozing out of this stir was smoke that hung over the houses like sweat.

Across the road at the traffic lights Trigger spotted a stretch of grass, and it was as much as I could do to hold him until the light changed to green, then Trigger made for it. Before I could dismount, a man came hurrying:

'You can't 'ave your 'orse on 'ere.'

We were on Shepherd's Bush Green and this was the keeper. I rode along Holland Park Avenue towards Notting Hill Gate. Trigger was ravenously hungry. The oats bought at High Wycombe had long since been eaten. A double stream of traffic, all motorised, was moving both ways. I kept near the kerb. Pedestrians whom I asked, when we were stopped by traffic lights, were so surprised at my question that they could hardly speak. They had not the slightest idea where food for a horse could be bought. Some of them looked frightened when I spoke to them and everybody was in a hurry. The first genuine fellow-feeling for Trigger came from a very small and very dirty boy who was peeping through some railings. He had his face between two iron rails looking at Trigger as I tethered him before going into a telephone kiosk to see if I could find the address of a corn merchant. I got out my moist sponge and bathed Trigger's eyes and face to refresh him. The boy, the only person who was not in a hurry, watched me with astonishment:

'What are you doing?'

'I'm washing his face.'

The boy's own face between his two dirty hands which were gripping the rails would have served as a perfect model for an artist who wished to paint sympathy and pity, mingled with horror. He sighed as he looked at the poor horse.

'Are you goin' to wash 'is 'ands?'

Suddenly Trigger neighed. I heard the sound of trotting hoofs. A costermonger with a pony and a dainty four-wheeled cart was turning into a side street. I mounted quickly and overtook him. The cockney scratched his chin trying to think where I could get oats in that part of London:

' 'arf a mo'. I know a plyce. There's a lydy keep a pet shop next to that eyetalian's plyce...' He told me how I could get to it. 'You're a northcountryman?' I told him that I had come from Yorkshire.

'Gorblimey! You cum all that bleedin' way wi' 'im?'

'We've taken our time. Twelve days.'

At the pet shop Trigger drank two buckets of water and I laid in a stock of oats and bran to last at least two days. Back in the traffic stream again, buses, vans and cars were moving bumper to bumper. At Victoria Gate we turned into Hyde Park and rode in pleasanter surroundings as far as Hyde Park Corner. I had planned to have lunch at my club. Reporters met me there and within an hour of my arrival at the Savage Club pictures of me and Trigger were appearing on the streets in the evening newspapers.

The climax of our ride to London was followed by an anticlimax. The reporters had asked me many questions but not one of them had asked me where we were going to sleep that night. I tried to follow the example of Trigger. He was carefree but I was worried, not forgetting the night at White

City. I rode him back to Rotten Row. There at any rate he could have his feet on soft ground. We had not been there long when an officer of the Royal Horse Guards came to me.

'Is this the horse you've ridden to London in thirteen days, sleeping rough?'

He looked Trigger over and said, 'Well I must compliment you on the condition of your horse.'

No guardsman ever stuck out his chest more than I did on receiving such a compliment from such a horseman.

'Where is he going to sleep tonight?'

'I don't know. Last night we slept under a tree at White City.'

'Bring him to Knightsbridge Barracks. We'll put him in Hannibal's box.' Hannibal had gone to the Horse of The Year show.

'Ask for Trooper Richards. Your horse will be given all that he needs.'

'Lucky, lucky Trigger!' I said, patting his crooked mane when we were alone again. 'Tonight you will be eating royal oats with the Queen's horses . . '

And to whom was I indebted for this royal hospitality?

'To my horse.'

My horse shied and drew back at the gates of Knightsbridge Barracks. He mistrusted the large half-circle of heavy iron plate which is embedded in the cobbles. At last after some high-spirited prancing he stepped over it and presently we rode into what at first seemed to be a long street. On one side were stables, on the other barrack rooms: Walking on the pavement were men in khaki field dress. The uniforms, like the pavement, were dull, drab almost, but through the open barrack room doors bright colours were bursting out into the street – vivid scarlet, deep blue, yellow, gold. Hanging from high pegs were breastplates and helmets of flashing steel and glittering brass, dyed sheepskins and rows of brilliant uniforms. By the lockers between polished saddles and bridles I could see men polishing and cleaning and chatting with each other. But Trigger could see the sleek necks of the black chargers craning over the half doors of their loose-boxes.

Trooper Richards came to me in his khaki field dress. Without helmet he did not appear tall and when he spoke to me I had another shock. He had a Yorkshire accent. Somehow, when thinking of Life Guards, and The Blues, I had always imagined that they were different from ordinary men. If I had ever spoken to one of these magnificent breast-plated men on horseback with his gleaming sword I would have expected to hear a cavalier accent. And here was a fairly broad Yorkshire accent! And yet why not? These men are recruited from all over the British Isles. Trooper Richards told me that his first name was Will.

Will led Trigger on to deep fresh straw in a loose-box. Trigger's legs went back and he at once made water and I knew that he was happy. The loose-box was the first in the row and over it on the wall on a plaque was the proud name: HANNIBAL.

From the next box a shiny black head craned out, looking at Trigger. Trooper Richards said, 'That's the charger that rides by the side of the Queen in royal processions.'

Before leaving the barracks I watched the busy polishing and chatted with other troopers, and I talked to a group of officers, Colonel Meredith Hardy and the Hon. Captain Beaumont of the Life Guards, and Major Hopkinson, squadron leader of The Blues. Walking alone through the big gates I stood in the street and waited for a bus.

I felt lonely. When a man has lived with a horse, eaten with a horse, swum with a horse, slept with a horse, travelled alone with a horse for months on end – hundreds of miles – the world seems empty without him. I could no longer hear his footsteps by my side.

It was strange too for me at my club to be sleeping in a bedroom and using furniture. For a long time my saddle-bags had been my wardrobe. Now I had three tall, roomy mahogany wardrobes and I did not need them. It felt strange even to use a chair and a table. My finger nails were torn, my fingers calloused with holding the reins, my jacket roughly mended; my boots were so badly worn and cracked by sun and rain I was ashamed to place them outside my bedroom door to be cleaned. But sun-tanned, weather-beaten, I fell asleep instantly when I got into bed with the chimes of Big Ben in my ears.

What was that! I sat up in bed. The clip-clop of horses' hoofs! I jumped out of bed and looked out of the wide open window. Daylight was coming over the skyline of Whitehall, the trees of St James's Park were still, and there below along the Mall two palace horses were drawing an empty wagonette with two coachmen in top hats on the box. They were driving round the park for exercise. The wagonette lamps were still lit. How lovely! Here in the very heart of the British Empire and Commonwealth was this horse-drawn vehicle with its lighted lamps. How lovely the sound of the horses' hoofs, the leisurely clip-clop in the quiet park between Whitehall and the Palace. For me nothing could be seen or heard more symbolical of peace and security than this quiet exercise of horses. Here I was at the very centre of power of the greatest Empire that has ever risen in history and which is changing into something new and yet remaining curiously the same, and here at the centre. at the very heart. horses have a place. an honoured place. The buildings which I could see emerging from the dawn were not ruins. They are still in use. And that day would echo in the Mall the feet of the chargers of the old guard and the new.

Lucky, lucky Britain! Lucky, lucky me! Lucky, lucky Trigger! A country that is free, and still has room ... for horses.

Leaning on that window-sill I felt again to be living a dream, a fairy tale. But it is true! True!

Along that avenue a real queen rides *on horseback*.

CHAPTER NINE

Picardy

I left England for the continent with Trigger without any definite plan beyond an intention to reach the Mediterranean before winter. British Railways had agreed to transport my horse from Folkestone to Boulogne if I would pay £4 for the hire of a box on the voyage and £14 for his fare. But we were held up at Folkestone by formalities. In the year of my birth it was easier to get a horse across the Channel than a car. Today a passenger on horseback is as rare as a motorist was then. The forms I had to fill up would make a bulging dossier. I even had to get an export licence from the Board of Trade because my horse was under £120 in value, and the standard printed application form for this licence asked such questions as, 'Method of packing, Quantity, Is it going by post?' A bulky envelope from the Animal Health Division of the Ministry of Agriculture and Fisheries contained many numbered and lettered forms and printed copies of 'Statutory Instruments'. The ministries of each European country require for a horse certificates of health, and of origin endorsed by a chamber of commerce. From France I received by post a long questionnaire required by the *Union Nationale Interprofessionnelle du Cheval* in Paris, and later a bill for sixty-five francs to cover the fee for a temporary permit with the visa of the French Ministry of Agriculture for the horse. One of the questions asked by this form was, 'The address where the horse will be stationed in France?' As Trigger and I are constantly on the move and we sleep in fields and woods by the wayside what answer could I give to this?

Poor Trigger! We stood on the quay at last and he was asking himself, 'What's going to happen now?' We were waiting to board the small cargo ship *Dorset Coast*. His ears

54

were swivelling and tuning-in to the confused marine noises – bells, shouts, whistles, sirens, and the rattle of winches. He had to be forced into a narrow box and shut in. He could see out through a slot and he looked at me questioningly. Poor Trigger! He neighed piteously as he was lifted higher than the mast. I held my breath. I knew that his weight was exactly half a ton and there was the heavy box. What if the cable broke? I carried my saddlebags up the gangway and joined him at once on deck. For the first time he did not take the mint-sweet I offered to him. It fell from his mouth. For me it was a familiar and pleasant sensation to feel the movement of the deck of a ship under my feet but for Trigger it was terrifying. I stood by his head where he could see out of his box, the harbour was moving away, the propellers thrashed, the coast of Britain receded. Water, water everywhere...

He was not the only horse aboard. Another, in a box by his side, a race-horse, was bound for Switzerland across France by rail accompanied by a groom. In just under three hours we entered the calm waters of Boulogne harbour. Presently a crane lifted Trigger in his box on to the quay where I at once drew the bolts. The door fell down with a crash. Trigger emerged into the sunlight on foreign soil.

The customs officials wanted papers and also a cash deposit of thirty-seven per cent of the value of the horse. Trigger was puzzled when he heard me talking in French. For the first time since leaving Folkestone harbour he took his eyes off his surroundings and looked at me. The certificate of health signed by an English veterinary surgeon was waved aside as useless. They now required a certificate signed by a French veterinary officer. The various fees and the cash deposit were quoted to me at first in old francs – '*anciens francs*' – thousands and thousands! I was almost in a state of panic until I realised that a new franc was worth a hundred old francs. Trigger wanted to make off at once in search of grass but we had to wait on the quay two hours for the French vet. When he came he examined Trigger quickly, hurried into his office, signed a certificate and collected his fee. I showed Trigger the printed yellow form and translated it for him into English:

'LAISSEZ-PASSER No 1561. The veterinary inspector of the customs office has examined at three o'clock today a white horse, Arab, 12 years old, from Great Britain and hereby declares that this merchandise has been found healthy and well preserved and is fit to eat.'

Finally we were free, Trigger no longer held in bond as 'merchandise'. I put my foot in the stirrup and mounted on French soil with all the continent of Europe before me. And it was my birthday – sixty-seven. My horse beat the race-horse out of Boulogne harbour. The groom had willingly agreed to wait for an endorsement of his horse's visa by a forwarding agency in Boulogne and pay the fee. I had jibbed at this additional piece of bureaucracy although the customs officials had said that it was necessary. Trigger and I did not need any 'Forwarding agency'. The groom of the race-horse would have to wait until the next day for endorsement as the forwarding office was now closed.

Happy Trigger now! His friend Bill singing Trigger's favourite song that goes so well to the clip-clop of his hoofs: 'There's a tavern in the town, in the town...' I translated it and sang it for Trigger in French.

Il y a un café dans la ville, dans la ville
Ou mon amant se faufile, se faufile,
Il boit son vin et ne pense jamais à moi...

I rode into Boulogne and stopped at a bar. 'It's my birthday,' I reminded Trigger. 'You are my only guest. We'll celebrate.' I tethered Trigger under the arch of the Rue de l'Amiral-Bruix and went into a bar.

'I want a bottle of the best champagne you've got, and a bucket or a large bowl.'

'You are not going to drink champagne from a bucket?' exclaimed the proprietress.

'No. It's for my horse.'

She closed her eyes and threw up her hands:

'Oh! Les Anglais!'

But Trigger declined the champagne, quite politely – he had not acquired the taste – 'no thanks, I'd rather not, if you don't mind'. I emptied a good ration of oats into the bucket and poured the champagne into the oats. Trigger bit deep into the oats and presently raised his face and without ceasing to masticate looked at me as much as to say, 'Hum! I rather like this. *Veuve Clicquot* did you say? Not bad.'

I was sixty-seven. I could not believe it. While Trigger basted himself with his champagne-oats my birthday had reminded me of a meeting I had had with a Chelsea Pensioner who was on holiday in Folkestone. We drank pints of beer together and chatted, he spoke to me patronisingly and I was looking up to him and treating him with the respect due to an old man from a younger man. His was a venerable presence in the pub, in his uniform with a row of medals, his grey hair and his stout stick.

'By the way, how old are you now?' I asked him as I was leaving him.

'Sixty-five.'

He was two years younger than myself!

'It's all propaganda,' I said to Trigger. 'Who says I'm sixty-seven? Who says you are twelve? We don't believe it, do we?'

'Hurrrrrh!' He blew oats into the air.

I began to sing 'My old Shako' – Time has entitled me to sing this. I was a volunteer soldier in 1914 – so 'Ten, twenty, thirty, forty, *fifty* year-r-r-s ago!' . . .

Now that we had reached France, before riding to the Mediterranean I had made up my mind to revisit the battlefields of Picardy, the battlefields I knew as a young soldier. So instead of taking the *grande route* to Paris I turned east and took the road to St Omer. Trigger did a few *salomes* as a salute to the champagne when I tested him on the white line. But I turned back. Before leaving Boulogne I decided to make good my kitty by sketching and selling my pictures. The cost of crossing the Channel, the veterinary fees and the customs deposit had made rather a hole in my funds. The first sketch I did I sold at once to the owner of the Café de l'Aurore. Several more rapid sketches and sales followed, portraits in charcoal sprayed with fixative. I was so happy I decided to stay overnight in Boulogne. A little way along the road out of Boulogne Trigger found a patch of grass behind some hoardings and there we slept. Up early next day I was drinking coffee with a glass of cognac at six o'clock in the morning without any policeman having any right to interfere. Britain would do well to adopt the French system of catering before the decimal system.

On the road to St Omer we slept the first night in a field at La Capelle and the second night in the open at the cross-roads of Harlette. I had chosen this part of the year to escape the heat of summer and to have time to get to the Mediterranean before winter. Fodder, also, is more plentiful after the harvest and on horseback one can ride over the stubble. I had very carefully chosen my equipment because I was making the journey almost without money. I had sewn two long waterproof sheets of nylon fabric together, the top sheet longer, about four feet longer, than the bottom sheet. Between these two sheets I slept, rolled in my blanket, with my saddle and saddlebags behind my head. If it rained during the night, without getting up I could throw the extra length of the upper sheet over my head and over my saddle-bags and cover all my equipment. To prevent the wind from lifting this extra flap or blowing it off I had sewn a pocket at each corner of the flap and into these pockets at night I put my boots. My artist's easel, when I was riding, was folded half size. It stuck out a few inches from the top of my saddlebag like a machine-gun. At night I laid the folded easel in the grass by my head. If it started to rain and I threw the flap over my head and the saddlebags, in order to breathe comfortably, I erected three legs of the easel, folded half size, by the side of my head – this I could do without getting up – and passed over the top of the three-legged easel a loop made of a leather thong sewn to the flap. It could rain cats and dogs and I didn't care a damn. Trigger had no problem at all, he was covered by nature from his tail to the tip of his nose and the wind could not blow his covering off; happily, like myself he had lived a hard life and loved the open air.

While having supper at the *estaminet* called *Au Carrefour d'Harlette* I remembered other French *estaminets* with less prosaic names. For instance, *Entrons ici il pleut là-bas,* and another – actually in the same street and directly opposite – *On est mieux ici qu'en face.*

On our way through the French countryside Trigger kept stopping to take a good look around. He often sees things before I do. We travel with four eyes and four ears and his ears and eyes are better than mine. I had been looking forward to showing Trigger France but I soon began to realise that it was he who was showing me – a hare, cattle, a pheasant in a distant wood, a tumbril on the skyline. There were no fences, and we hardly ever kept to the road. We both enjoyed the mad gallops over the stubble. Grand it was to be on horseback galloping over fields in northern France. The route we might take later was a question left to the future. We might go west through Perpignan to Spain or east along the Riviera to Italy. I might even drop the reins at Narbonne and let Trigger chose. We might even visit both Spain and Italy. Meanwhile we were on our way to the battlefields of Picardy.

We had arrived in the little hamlet of Bayenghem-les-Seninghem at six o'clock in the morning. Halting at the sun-lit crossroad I wondered if I could buy some oats. There was not a soul in sight, our shadows were long, all was peaceful, the cream-coloured road bathed in warm sunlight. In the stillness and silence I heard the sound of shutters being opened. A woman leaned out of the bedroom window of a large house with wrought iron gates and spoke to me in French:

'I believe I know who you are. You are an Englishman. And you are going to Bavinchove.'

I was astounded. How did she know this? At first I had the feeling that I was reading this in a book. The situation was familiar in a curious way. It was something I had read – a foreigner on horseback on his way to a battlefield, a woman leaning out of a bedroom window. Shades of *La Chartreuse de Parme*, of course! Stendhal. Fabrice del Dongo. I was about to ask her how she knew who I was when she continued:

'My husband is cousin to Germain Beck who lives at Bavinchove. We have heard that you have written to him and that he is expecting you. We have been listening for horse's hoofs.'

True. I had written a letter. It was at that *domaine* at Bavinchove where I was once billeted when my regiment was behind the firing line for a rest. I had received a reply from Germain. The old *patron* and *patronne,* M. et Mme. Beck-Minne were dead. Germain, the grandson, was now *patron.*

The fair head had disappeared from the sunlight into the bedroom and presently I heard the iron gates opening. She was in her dressing-gown:

'When I opened the window I said to my husband, *"Regarde ce cavalier!"* '

I rode into a spacious courtyard where four dogs chained to the walls began to bark. The woman's husband, Monsieur Auguste Thuillier, invited me into the house. Trigger was given a drink of water, some oats and hay and I sat down to a sumptuous breakfast with wine. Auguste gave me the address of his son who owns a farm on the road to Bavinchove. It is remarkable how interrelated are the farming families of the Pas de Calais. Later, in St Omer, at another crossroad a car drew up and a woman spoke to me: 'You are looking for the way to Bavinchove. I am the sister of Raymonde, wife of Monsieur Thuillier. I am Yvonne, wife of Paul Duthoit. We have a farm at Campagne Wardrecques near Arcques. It is on the way to Bavinchove. Please stay with us tonight.' I accepted the invitation on condition that I was allowed to sleep with Trigger in one of their fields. By the time I had reached Bavinchove I had met a score of peasants all related to Germain Beck and everybody in the neighbourhood knew of my arrival. Everywhere there was a popping of corks. 'A drink of wine?' At Campagne Wardrecques an old lady wanted to meet me and I was asked to call on her at once because she went to bed early. Surrounded respectfully by all her family of several generations and by neighbours who had squeezed into the house she uncorked a bottle of old wine with her own ivory fingers.

At the farm in Bavinchove, Germain and his wife welcomed me. His son Pascal and daughter Odile had met me on the road with their bicycles to show me the way. As if I did not know the way to this place that I had loved fifty years before! But I greatly missed the dear old patron and his wife, M. and Mme. Beck-Minne. And I missed Adrienne, the buxom daughter a few years older than myself with whom I had flirted in a jocular way and whom I had helped to milk the cows. 'Adrienne is coming here to meet you,' said Germain. 'She has a farm near Dunkirk.'

Adrienne arrived in a car driven by her son. There she stood facing me, and under her arm was a framed picture, a water-colour of the farm at Bavinchove that I had painted and signed, 'Billy'. Her hair was grey, her face thin and careworn, her hand shrunken, she was bent, her heavy body leaning on a stick. Rheumatism. Poor Adrienne! I burst into tears.

Trigger and I stayed three days, sleeping at night in one of the fields, and I did another picture of the farm and signed it with the date 1964. The farm buildings were the same but had been added to. There is now a garage and shed for tractor implements. The horses have gone, and the trap in which I used to ride with old Monsieur and Madame Beck to church. But the fields are the same. And the cows have the same leisurely gait on their way to graze. '*Allez! Allez à la pâture!*' The mayor of Bavinchove came to greet me in the field where I slept. One morning early I heard shots in the field and saw three men walking slowly along the hedge. A man with a bandolier of cartridges came to me and introduced himself 'I am the son-in-law of Adrienne: and this is my son.' When we left this French farm, Madame

Beck gave me a *casse-croûte* for the road – a bag full of bread, cheese, sausage, tomatoes, and hard-boiled eggs.

We rode to Hazebrouck. The roads and the railway brought back nostalgic memories. Route marches with full pack, railway *wagons*, '40 *hommes, 8 chevaux.' Estaminets* with Flemish stoves that extend out into the middle of the tiled floor, the dialect of the Pas de Calais, the *patois* – '*Quoi que shay sha?*' – '*Shay vray.*' I was now warned of a new hazard by the peasants. 'Don't let your horse graze on the roadside by fields where potatoes have been cultivated. The plants have been sprayed with a poisonous pest chemical.' It was market day in Hazebrouck. I bought a new blanket and felt much warmer that night when we slept at Haverskerque on our way to Béthune.

Living with a horse night and day, travelling together far from home, one gets to know one another very intimately. I tried to make it clear to Trigger that I did not wish him to look upon me as his master but as his friend. Our relationship might not meet with the approval of some horsemen but it works very well with Trigger and me. For instance, if I accidentally bump against him I say, 'I'm sorry! I beg your pardon,' and he understands. He knows when I am unhappy and he tries to cheer me up by his little gambols which always make me laugh. A happy horse is one of the gayest companions. How happy we both were when galloping over the stubble but I could feel that he was surprised that our journey was taking us such a long way and his poor feet and back must have suffered sometimes although he did not show it. He was obviously puzzled when he heard me talking to people in French. He soon began to pick up French words such as the words for oats, water, sugar lumps, and French words of endearment. A horse understands a lot more than some people imagine although he is silent and not so demonstrative as a dog. I could sense his impatience when I stopped to read newspapers about Rhodesia and Vietnam. It was as if he was trying to say, 'Why not take more interest in what is happening here and now?' He signals to me with his ears and his feet and I understand the sounds he makes. When he is tired he touches my toe with his nose and I dismount at once and walk by his side. Walking up a steep hill in the hot sun I have sometimes snatched a small leafy branch from a tree and fanned his face and he has closed his eyes in gratification. Sometimes when I am walking in front, holding the reins, he bites my back or gives me a good butt and I know that he is doing that because he loves me. When he becomes bored by the slow pace he pushes me and I mount again and he begins to trot. If he hears a rustle of paper he slows down, turns his head and I give him a mint goody. He has a better memory than I have and sometimes he has to remind me which pocket I have put them in. He can untie knots with his teeth, open doors and gates, and while we were sleeping in a field at the Carrefour d'Harlette, he turned on a tap in the night. I thought it was raining. I am sure I heard him chuckle when I got up to turn it off.

We were travelling east towards the battlefields. Trigger seemed to want to follow the birds and go south. And the thought came to me that horses would never go to battlefields if they were not driven there by men. There are better fields than battlefields: peaceful green fields, clothed with clover and lucerne.

At the village of Wisques a woman came to us out of a crowd outside a new church which was being consecrated. She patted Trigger and said to me, 'I will ask the priest to say a prayer for you.' I thanked her and said, 'Ask him to pray for my horse.'

If horses prayed – and perhaps they do – this would be one of Trigger's prayers:

> Lead me over soft pine needles.
> Deliver me from the *grande route*.
> Give me trees to rub against,
> Trees with low branches to scratch my back,
> Bushes to back into to scratch my belly.
> Give me time to graze and roll.

O deliver me from amateur veterinaries
And those who 'know all about horses'.
Bless Bill for taking off my blinkers.
And now remove the blinkers from Bill,
So that he can see the open gates
And the luscious pasture.
Help him to stop smoking.
Chewing clover is much better.
I know he really wants to stop.
It is such a nuisance for him,
Losing his pipe, shopping for matches,
Fumbling with only two hands and a horse.
O preserve me from lands where they eat horses . . .

Entering the town of Béthune we had our first accident
– fortunately a minor one. Some workmen were demolishing
a house. All of a sudden they dumped a heavy load of
masonry from an upper storey. It fell with a crash into the
street. Trigger shied against the wall of the house opposite
and ripped the nearside saddlebag from top to bottom. But
even before I had dismounted to console Trigger and to pick
up all the things that had fallen out of my saddlebag, I saw
through the open window of a nearby building some skins
hanging up to dry. It was a tannery! What a fortunate co-
incidence! I tried to buy but was given a large sheet of
leather and in the square of Béthune I sat down on a wicker
chair outside a café with a glass of wine and mended my
saddlebag by sewing a big patch of leather on it. While I was
so engaged a man came to me and introduced himself as
Augustin Delhaye, an *avocat* at the bar of Béthune. He
invited me and Trigger to the local riding club and led the
way by driving his car slowly to *Les Jardins des Sports*. He
introduced me to the president of the club and we drank
wine together. Delhaye told me that after the battle of Waterloo the English came there and his family welcomed them on
that same land. Trigger was put in a box on deep straw and
given oats. At a banquet that night I was made an honorary
member of the S.H.R., the rural horse-riding clubs of France
and the president gave me an enamel badge. I was invited
to stay there with Trigger as long as we liked.

The clip-clop of Trigger's footsteps echo on London's pavement.

Running repairs on the road-side. I always carry a full kit for repairing leather, canvas, and clothing, and I am never without a few horse-shoe nails.

Morning after a night in the open. I always saddle my horse barefoot. Dew-soaked boots take a long time to dry.

Next day I rode to Festubert where as a young soldier in the First World War I went into action for the first time. It was with nostalgia that I revisited those flat low fields below Givenchy Ridge where once thousands of men crouched out of sight and the fields were unploughed sighing wastes of grasses bending in the wind, swept clean by machine guns. I found the sunken road which was once our front line and again I stood in the exact spot where No Man's Land used to be. I felt lonely standing there. It was at this spot that I once arranged an unofficial armistice to collect the wounded and the dead.

The sunken road is now little more than a dry ditch overgrown with grass. Trigger was nibbling the seeds from the tops of the tall grasses and watching me with curiosity out of the corner of his eye. I crouched down in the sunken road and peered over the waving grasses at what used to be enemy territory occupied by another force, hostile and lethal. The distant farmhouses were no longer in ruin, the shattered thickets were again in full leaf, but the contours of the low hills were the same . . . I looked for a long time at that haunted landscape .

On my return to Béthune I rode into a narrow street where during the First World War an *estaminet* was converted into a temporary brothel for soldiers with local women recruited for their pleasure. I had visited the brothel myself, but now, like the trenches that have disappeared, the brothel is no longer there.

From Béthune I rode to the Somme where I remember the quick thrill of movement in open fighting with the trenches left behind. My mind went back to the tramp of feet with my comrades on the road: 'Left! Left! Left right left! I had a good home and I left. Left! Left! I had a good home and I left.' Surveying the scene from the saddle I thought of my old comrades who have left this world of time and space and things that are material . . .

> 'They are all gone into the world of light
> And I sit lingering here.
> Their very memory is fair and bright
> And my sad thought does clear.

> And yet as angels in some brighter dreams
> Call to the soul when man doth sleep,
> So some thoughts transcend our wonted themes
> And into glory peep...'[1]

Just before entering Amiens I rode through a big old archway into a farmyard which is very old and very French. It is an ancient building called 'Le Pigeonnier'. Although it was Sunday morning and early, the farmyard was crowded with people buying eggs, milk, chickens, and the plump *patronne* was serving them and joking with them. This romantic old building on the main road to Paris once stood almost alone surrounded only by a few cottages and fields. Now with the growth of population it is in a built-up area of Amiens. The scene was so colourful and animated it might have been a stage setting for an episode in *The Scarlet Pimpernel*. Although modern automobiles were passing at speed along the road outside I could imagine at any moment seeing a coach or a cart or a tumbril entering the courtyard through the ancient archway into the straw-littered courtyard. Madame Pécourt, the patronne, refused to accept money from me for as many oats as Trigger could carry, and a great fuss was made of my horse who drank greedily at the enormous water trough.

News of the Englishman on a horse with saddlebags loaded up for a long journey had spread. People on the roadside shouted greetings and encouragement:

'Le chapeau!'
'C'est formidable!'
'Courage!'
'Bonne continuation!'
'Vive l'Angleterre!'

That ride to the Somme through Bruay en Artois and St Pol, and down the steep hill into Doulens was full of memories for me. The hospitality of the French, rich and poor, was warm. One big farm with stone pillars and a vaulted roof had stables as big as a church, and I drank hot

[1] I have come across these lines somewhere but I have never been able to trace the writer.

milk in farmhouses where the father and his tall sons kissed each other on the cheeks at breakfast time.

South of Amiens at Dury we were able to leave the *grande route* again and ride along quiet country roads and it was here that I met de Witte. He was travelling north with a horse-box. When he saw us he stopped and invited us to stay the night at his farm, Campreux, near Conty. Darkness fell before we got there, and drenching rain. His son came out to meet us by car. 'Follow the telephone wire at the first road on the right,' he said. We did so but there was no sign of a house or any buildings at all. We had ridden into a lonely deep hollow. Obviously something was wrong. Trigger was tired, and I cannot bear to hear the sigh of a horse. I drew up and in the darkness shouted at the top of my voice, 'De Witte! Renaud de Witte!' My voice echoed in the hollow but there was no response. I blew my horn, then returned the way we had come. Half an hour later on the main road we met the car again and this time we were led to Campreux where Trigger found shelter and I dined with the family. Young de Witte had not counted a narrow road which was the first on the right and which also had a telephone wire and posts.

We were in darkness again the next night when we arrived at a place suggested by de Witte for our next stop. He had given me the name of M. de Hardivilliers. I inquired for this person in the tiny village. A woman said, 'Ah, you mean the vicomte de Hardivilliers. He lives at the château. Go up the road past the cross and through the wood.' A half moon had risen and the windows of the château were lit up. The Viscountess welcomed us. Her husband was out hunting but was expected back at any time. She was astonished when I declined the offer of a bedroom, explaining to her why I always slept with my horse. Trigger and I were already lying in the grass near the château when footsteps approached and a woman's voice whispered, 'He's asleep.' I sat up. 'Wouldn't you like something warm, some hot soup?' the voice asked. I thanked her, told her that I had had supper on the way. I was sleeping with my horse because he was tired and he would not lie down until I came to him and I wanted him to have a good rest for the journey next day. 'Then you must have breakfast with us tomorrow,' said the Viscount, and in the morning while Trigger grazed I had breakfast in the Château.

From the Château de Monceaux we were able to get within a day's ride of Paris without using the main road. We passed Beauvais and slept by a haystack at Puiseux le Hauberger. When eventually we had to use the main road again for a short distance the dreariness was striking. The stink, noise, and draughts from the passing cars and lorries were bad enough but the litter that fouled the grass on each side made it disgusting and even dangerous for a horse – broken bottles, tin cans, plastic containers, that had come from the towns. Near Saint Brice we left the *grande route* again and soon after passing through Groslay, I caught my breath with excitement. There in the far distance on the horizon was a thin spire that dwarfed everything else on the flat skyline. The Eiffel Tower.

We stayed a week in Paris. Renaud de Witte had given me a note of introduction to Colonel de Roland of the *Cercle de l'Étrier* in the Bois de Boulogne. I could have stayed there with my horse – we were given a cordial welcome when we visited that most famous riding club – but on entering Paris via St Denis we had already been invited to stay in a *manège* at Neuilly: 'Make yourself at home here and stay as long as you like, *vous êtes chez vous!*' In Paris I accumulated quite a fund, sketching on the banks of the Seine, or in the early morning around Les Halles painting the colourful scenes in the fruit and vegetable markets, my pictures selling on sight. Trigger surprised everybody by his good behaviour in the swift and closely packed traffic, he was cool, nonchalant, phlegmatic; one newspaper describing him said that he gave a kick at those who failed to recognise his right of way, but this was an exaggeration. I did, however, think that he was becoming *blasé* when on the first morning we rode along the Avenue de la Grande Armée, Place de l'Etoile, Champs Elysées, and feeling thirsty when we arrived at the Place de la Concorde he mounted the steps and drank at the fountain. Everywhere the Parisians crowded around and petted

Trigger, exclaiming, '*Qu'il est beau! Qu'il est mignon!*'
Trigger was the only horse in the Paris streets. We climbed
the steep hill to the church of the Sacré Coeur and visited
the artists of Montmartre who gave a cheer when they saw
Trigger. In the Bois de Boulogne on the soft soil under the
trees other riders greeted us, the men taking off their hats
to me with a sweeping gesture. *L'Éperon*, the leading French
glossy magazine for horse-lovers commissioned an illustrated
article from me. French television invited me to Rue
Cognacq-Geay where Trigger remained as cool as a cucum-
ber when I rode him through the entrance, up the corridor,
into a lift, and into a studio on the third floor. The com-
mentator, François Ponchelet, said to viewers, 'This is the
first time a horse has been in the studio.' Trigger basked
in the warm light, began to doze and nearly fell asleep while
I was being interviewed and some of my sketches of Paris
were shown on television.

CHAPTER TEN

Touraine

Leaving Paris we crossed the Seine and made for the Loire. We were up very early that first morning, saddlebags loaded, both of us in high glee. We rode through the Bois de Boulogne making for the Pont de Sèvres. The trees and ourselves cast very long shadows. Trigger frisked and danced. We were both so high-spirited I took off all the harness and of course Trigger bolted. He wanted to play *cache-cache* with me. We were so carefree we missed our way in the wood and came out at Suresnes. The bridge there crosses the Seine but I had to ride back along the bank for miles to get to the Pont de Sèvres and this was the worst bit of road we had travelled up to now in all our long journey. Heavy lorries were passing in both directions with only just room on the unevenly cobbled road for them to pass each other. There was no side-walk and between every tree on the river side were parked cars of employees who work at the factories on the banks. The steep camber of the cobbled surface bothered Trigger and the drivers of the lorries which were moving bumper to bumper and were unable to allow us much room. We could not get off the road or turn back.

When we had entered the Bois de Boulogne I had counted my money. I had twelve francs. The cost of living in Paris was very high. But when we got free from that awful road and rode up the hill from the Pont de Sèvres into the open country I counted my money again and I had fifty. I had sold some more sketches in the Bois and at Suresnes. That was how it was now. I was relying entirely on my sketching and was happy to find that my pictures sold easily and when in the mood I could work quickly. My charcoal sketches of the bridges over the Seine were popular, my impressions of the gargoyles of Notre Dame appealed to fewer, but fetched higher prices. Over the Rue d'Arcole the towers of Notre Dame seem to separate and suddenly a row of gargoyles leap out at you, long necks craning, jaws open, ears well back, and looking down into the Rue du Cloître, beasts and demons crane their necks, howling. They sit out horizontally without falling down as if the cathedral was their centre of gravity. Trigger, tethered, tuned his ears to the open doorway of the cathedral as I sketched. Out of the hush would suddenly issue a deep chord of music that ceased at once and a deep shuddering echo passed through the whole mass of masonry. Now a trumpet blast, some reedy pipe notes, muttering thunder sinking into a groan and silence. Trigger listened sphinx-like and sometimes I thought his own face looked like a gargoyle. I did not like parting with the paintings of Les Halles Centrales – what scenes! – the piles of wooden crates and baskets higher than the crowd, the pavement knee-deep in straw, wooden shavings and coloured tissue paper. The horns of the ladder-like *crochets* of the porters stuck up and moved about over the heads and on each side of the street were piles of cauliflowers, artichokes, asparagus, green grapes and water melons. Everybody smiled at Trigger but if I got in the way of the handcarts the porters yelled murderously and pushed me out of the way. No ceremony at that time in the morning in Paris. The funnel-like entrance to the Rue du Jour under the shadow of St Eustache was blocked with carts and motor vans. Engraved in stone over the entrance to the church was: *'Liberté, égalité, fraternité.'*

I was happy. I had lost weight, I took up the straps of my riding breeches another inch, and felt as fit as a fiddle. Mostly on my ride I did my own washing as best I could, drip-drying my shirts on a tree branch or even on the horse behind the saddle *en route*, but in Paris I had had time to wait for my stock of linen to be laundered for me. Once across the Seine we left the main road again and bypassed Versailles. The first night Trigger and I slept in the garden of a big house.

It rained heavily in the night and I dried my cape in the house while having breakfast in the morning. At midday when I arrived at Châteaufort I found that I had forgotten my cape. Jacques and Berthe Gosset who own a riding school at Châteaufort, offered to give me a lift in their car to fetch my cape. I felt disgraced. It was another lesson for me to be more careful when part of my equipment overflows into a house. Out in a field one can see whether anything is left on the ground.

It was Saturday. Jacques and Berthe spread a table at the open stable doors and we lunched in semi-open air. They wanted me to stay the night on their strip of pasture running along the back gardens of some houses. Trigger bounded with joy and rubbed himself on trees. Neighbours came from the houses to feed him with tit-bits. Sunday morning came warm and sunny with cocks crowing, three donkeys braying, horses neighing, ducks quacking, church bell tolling. We were now in the *département* of Seine-et-Oise. On our way south through the village the inhabitants competed with each other to welcome us, shopkeepers refused money when I went in for cheese and fruit, the woman from the café next door came into the shop to invite me to have a drink, Trigger was regaled with sugar lumps and biscuits. Everywhere doors and shutters were open and nearly every other building along the road was a bar or a café with chairs outside and tables under gaily coloured umbrellas. Sunday morning! And early! Shops open and cognac, wine and beer available, and all the variety of French *apéritifs* and liqueurs. O England! How different from that Sunday morning in Birmingham! *Certainly* they 'do things better in France'. Trigger grazed the fresh flowering clover while I flopped on a chair and began to paint and paint with a glass of wine at my elbow. How could I help it. And Trigger would not have minded how long we lingered there.

A little farther along the road south two young women caught up to us, running. *'Nous avons une grande prairie pour le cheval!'* Breathlessly they invited me to lunch. They were artists and lived about a mile away in a house buried in a grassy hollow where a dog and some goats wandered

in the wild grass. They uncorked a bottle of wine in the
sunlight and we drank wine together before going in for
lunch. In less than a minute Trigger's knees bent and he lay
down in the sun. 'This year, 1964, will be a good year for
wine,' they said. 'Not a lot, but good.'

That day we got only as far as Les Molliers, about ten
miles, where there is a *cercle hippique* and we were able to
sleep on the grass in the riding school paddock among the
hurdles. The old *palefrenier*, Robert Nardou, lives alone in
a small house with his pet cat that leaps and runs all over
his furniture. He insisted on giving me a meal, and in the
morning a *casse-croûte* for the road, as much as I could
carry – bread and butter, ham, sausage, eggs, biscuits and
cans of fruit juice.

We had got off the map again. I had to buy another one –
this time of Eure-et-Loir. The lovely French town of
Chartres was only twenty-seven kilometres away, but we did
not get to Chartres that day, Trigger's shoes were about
finished and I was lucky to find a farrier. The farrier had
tools rather different from those in England and he expected
me to hold Trigger's foot, providing me with a leather strap
to go over my shoulder. After that, Trigger and I slept in
an open prairie, near a sort of wild west settlement with
ramshackle buildings and broken automobiles.

Busy Chartres on the hilly banks of the Eure, its cathedral
in a blue sky, tempted me to linger, but for the sake
of Trigger within an hour we left its hilly streets and were
on our way south again towards Tours and the river Loire.

The *grande route* was hard to the feet and stank with
rubbish where automobiles had stopped. Motorists dump
rubbish anywhere. At one point a chimney sweep had
emptied his sack in the long grass. When I came out of a
café and rejoined Trigger he was a black horse. Not being
able to read maps, Trigger did not understand that the
grande route was the most direct way to Paris and the south.
He would have avoided Paris if it had not been for me. The
only time he was really happy there was in the Bois de

Boulogne or in Les Halles Centrales being fed with carrots and celery by the market porters. The water at the big fountain in the Place de la Concorde tasted no better than anywhere else. Trigger's preference was for the open countryside or visiting the big farms. At Warluis he saw a foal only one day old. While we were guests of M. de Witte he saw a dog riding on a donkey's back. That was clever, and a better show for Trigger than the sights of Paris. Both Trigger and I were happy to be under a clear open sky again in the rolling countryside.

On the way to La Bourdinière rain came for the first time in fifteen days while actually riding. I stopped and sat under an umbrella outside Les Routiers café. I was in no hurry had no appointments, no letters, no news from England. I stretched out my arms as far as they would go and let them come slowly back. In the mirror in the toilet my cheeks shone like rosy apples and I felt the glow of autumn all over my body. I had not much money and all Europe lay before me but I had my tubes of paint, my pencils and charcoal, my French was fluent, and the people I met were all friendly. In darkness we arrived at a village called Le Temple. *'Frappez à la porte blanche,'* said a woman when I began to look for a farm, and again we were met with warm hospitality. There was excitement on our arrival in the square at Bonneval. At the open door of le Petit Coin café the patron waved to me, shouted, almost commanded me to tether Trigger to the rail at the bottom of his steps. Fog came on our way to Châteaudun but lifted early. Unmistakable was the season now, the sun rising each morning like a dull tin plate in a colder mist with heavy dew. Trees on the roadside were weighed down with apples, the ground beneath strewn with windfalls. In the large town of Vendôme a tall elderly man, an ex-officer of the French dragoon guards wearing the ribbon of Commander of the Legion of Honour came to me in the square, invited me to his home where after a treble whisky we had lunch, and although he was seventy-nine years old he declared that he would accompany me on horse-back towards Tours. He went ahead of me in his car to St Anne, saddled and mounted his black mare, and ramrod erect he rode with me over the fields of stubble. He told me that he had been formerly head instructor at a military school of horsemanship.

That night Trigger and I halted early and slept at Le Paradis. And it was a paradise for us, a wide pasture sur-rounded by woods and extensive park land. Trigger was free to roam with abundant fresh sweet grass to eat, and *madame* from the big farmhouse came to the gate with coffee, cake and fruit for me. The *grande route* was as straight as an arrow for miles through the forest of Château-Renault. A wide grass verge ran alongside all the way to the town, soft for Trigger's feet. But the weather was changing now; heavy rain was falling. The narrow streets of Château-Renault were flooded.

But this rainstorm was as nothing compared with the gale and heavy rain the day I rode into Tours. The rain had be-gun in the morning and had gone on all day with the wind increasing in violence. As we approached the river Loire it seemed as if a battle was being fought out in the sky, winds south of the river and winds north of it attacking and counter-attacking and each trying to out-blow and out-rain the other. Clouds were changing direction, bits of blue sky appeared in the west and then in the south but the rain never ceased. I was wearing my monsoon cape, and oilskin fire-man's leggings over my riding breeches, but the wind drove the rain down my neck and under my cape where the reins came out over Trigger's withers – I had closed the arm-holes and held the reins under my cape. Normally my cape covers most of my saddlebags but the powerful gusts of wind blew it up and these were now soaked. In England I had never stopped for rain, had just ridden on regardless, other-wise we could not have got very far; but now I was driven to shelter with Trigger for several hours under the glass canopy of a café. We could not stay there all day so eventually I rode on, in the rain. We were riding down the steep hill into Tours when a young cyclist drew up and said,

'You can shelter at St Cyr. There are stables and horses. I am going there. Follow me.' He turned up a steep lane and in a few minutes we arrived. It is an ill wind that blows nobody any luck. Had it not been for the heavy gale I might never have met de Mieulle.

Roland de Mieulle, an ex-cavalry officer, tall, broad-shouldered and a passionate lover of horses, is director of the *Centre de Formation Equestre,* La Grenadière, St Cyr-sur-Loire. He is married to the daughter of the mayor of St Cyr, Louis Blot, and lives with his father-in-law in the mansion of the estate, La Grenadière. He has been a stormy petrel, a brave man whose political activities, adventurous and dangerous, have been of a type which would appeal to writers of romantic historical novels. He welcomed me, gave shelter for Trigger, and I dined with him, his five children, and his father and mother-in-law.

I slept with Trigger on straw in a shed with an iron roof on which the rain was drumming. When I awoke I heard a clock strike five, and Trigger was snoring by my side. I fell asleep again and awoke to hear the clock strike six. Trigger was now rustling in the straw to get up and presently was munching hay. The rain had stopped, a dog barked. Trigger stopping munching. We heard a gruff voice and the door opened. Switching on my torch, the beam lit up a man, a groom, who was speaking fast in dialect saying that he was only anxious about my horse. Wanting to help he brought water for Trigger, saying, *'Le chien n'est pas méchant.'* De Mieulle was up early. He was regretting that we had struck such bad weather. He showed me round the extensive estate which included a house on the slope over the Loire where Balzac wrote some of his books. Then he declared that he would ride with me across country on my next day's journey. He took no waterproof coat, saying that it never rained when he was riding. It did, but two servants caught us up by car at a crossroad in the forest with a raincoat for him and a cover for his horse. Before evening he put me on a road which enabled me to avoid the very heavy traffic on the bank of the Loire and left me.

My ride across France described a large arc westwards

almost as far as Nantes and then south-west via Poitiers. Rather to my surprise I had been invited to visit the Marquis de Meaulne at the Château de Landeronde. No doubt I have to thank Trigger for this. The Marquis is a great lover of horses. There Trigger and I rested for several days and Trigger was newly shod. From Anjou I had intended to pass through Limoges but winter came early with snow on the hills so I avoided the Massif Central and took the route through Angoulême, Périgueux, Bergerac, Agen, Toulouse, and Carcassonne.

The hospitality we met with everywhere was profoundly moving. Peasants and noblemen, rich and poor, the spirit was the same. In a humble cottage on the roadside I was sitting down to a meal of boiled chestnuts peeled, with butter, and goat's cheese, when there was a knock at the door and into the cottage burst a young man and woman with a basket containing a bottle of wine and all kinds of tasty, dainty things, from a neighbouring château, and they brought with them the compliments of the count and countess of Fonchais. One Sunday morning with little money in my pocket I arrived in a village square thinking how nice it would be to sit down to what we call in the north of England 'a Sunday dinner' – roast beef, Yorkshire pudding with a big jug of gravy, a rice pudding, and so on and so on, when from among the crowd that had gathered around Trigger a young man came with a card on which was written in French, 'You are invited to the Hotel des Voyageurs for a good meal, gratis.' The good meal started with an apéritif, then soup, *escargots* (bubbling in their shells with hot sauce, good! I like them), fish, meat, creamed potatoes, vegetables, salad, a choice of twelve different cheeses, an orange cut into the shape of a basket. Two different bottles of wine were placed before me and English cigarettes with the wish, '*Bon appétit.*' Then followed coffee and liqueurs. Meanwhile the patron had whispered, '*On va chercher du fourrage pour le cheval – et un abri,*' and his father, who was a saddler by occupation, was mending my saddle, sewing on the rings that had broken off. No wonder, after such a banquet, that I accompanied myself on a guitar which I found there and sang them a song like the troubadour I was becoming. Then the *patronne,* a charming blonde, produced a pencil, a rubber, a sharpener and cartridge paper and I made a sketch for them of their hotel.

While I was staying at the Château de Landeronde, the marquis gave a hunt dinner and from the many guests I received invitations to castles along the Loire. But one rainy night in the darkness on the road I thought that hospitality had forsaken us. I called at two farms and was refused accommodation. In each case it was the farmer's wife who stood at the door. Trigger and I were soaking wet, my hat was dripping, my cape too, and I was wearing my fireman's leggings. One said 'the farmer is away,' the other said, 'we haven't a suitable field.' Then I realised when we got on the road again that the women were afraid of me. I must have looked a fearsome figure to them in the dark and rain, a stranger, a foreigner unkempt and wet with a horse. 'Okay!' I said to Trigger, 'We'll sleep on the grass on the roadside as we have done before,' and we stopped a little farther on. During the night I was awakened by a voice and car headlights, *'Qu'est ce qu'il y a ici?'* – *'Qu'est ce que vous faites ici?'* Trigger got up. 'We're sleeping,' I said. 'It's all right.' Another car drew up and stopped. Presently eight cars and two lorries were stopped on the road where Trigger and I had settled for the night, all the drivers believing that an accident had taken place and that Trigger and I were the victims. When it had been explained to all of them that nothing was wrong and that we were sleeping there because it was the only place we could find, the traffic moved on again but not before some of the drivers had expressed pity for us, sleeping in the open. Little did they know how we pitied motorists shut in their cars. When they had all gone Trigger lay down again with a sigh of contentment. I awoke in the morning to find him happily backing into the prickly hedge to scratch himself. As soon as he saw me move he came up to me making figure eights with his head, then he shook it so vigorously that he appeared to have a dozen eyes gyrating in a circle. It made me laugh. He pushed his head against me, prodding with his upper lip at the packet of

apricot sandwich biscuits that I had taken out of my saddlebag.

On this long journey with Trigger I was beginning to learn
the real meaning of horse-sense. Each time we were approaching a village Trigger drew back. I had food in my saddlebag and a bottle of wine but I was thinking of a café or a
bar. Yes, I would go in for a drink and leave my best friend
outside. It sounds rather mean of me, put in that way, but
Trigger preferred to remain outside. I know that Trigger
does not consider me to be a mean man. It is more likely
that he thinks that I am foolish. I should not leave my best
friend outside. I should *stay outside with him*. Sometimes
when he knows that I am about to leave him he holds on
to my coat sleeve with his teeth as much as to say, 'Don't
leave me, Bill. Stay with me.' Another thing I have noticed
is that when it suddenly comes on to rain and I am hurrying
to get out my monsoon cape and at the same time covering
up the saddle, fiddling with straps and buckles, and trying
to hold so many things at once, I may get impatient and
swear in English, 'Oh hell! Drop the lot.' Then Trigger looks
at me with round eyes as much as to say 'Why don't you?'
A rainstorm came while we were riding through a deep forest.
I was pressing on towards a village that I had seen on the
map. The girth strap broke and as I was fumbling in my
saddlebag the saddle, saddlebags and the whole darned lot
began to slide down on to the road. And I am sure that
Trigger helped it down by shaking himself deliberately. I
got Trigger and his harness under a tree and before mending
the broken strap I sat down with my sandwiches and my
bottle of wine and enjoyed my meal in the fresh air, Trigger
meanwhile cropping the nearby grass. And that was just how
Trigger wanted it. I had never smacked my lips more over
a meal than I did that day in the deep forest in the rain.
The food and the wine tasted better than anything I had
ever enjoyed in a café or at a bar. I began to wish that we
could ride across France on soft leaves and grass as in this
forest, and as I was lunching *alfresco* I thought of what De
Mieulle had told me. In France they have nearly finished

a map showing how you can ride a horse across the whole of France without going on a hard road. Now *that* is horse-sense! I am sure that Trigger would help me to make a map like that for England.

When I had finished my meal and had mended the girth strap we rode on through the forest swishing through the fallen leaves and when we came to the village I rode straight through without stopping at a bar.

Trigger was full of zest but he was getting hungry again and we had no more oats. Once again a miracle happened. A man in a car caught up with us bringing oats for Trigger in a bucket. He emptied them into my oats bag – enough for two days. He introduced himself: 'Le Chevalier Éleveur de l'Ile Perdue.' He had seen us pass his house. He gave me another address in a town a few miles ahead, saying, 'You could shelter there and stop overnight.' Meanwhile on the opposite side of the road a woman had discreetly pushed her café door ajar, obviously hoping that I would come in, and on the road a mother superior stopped to say to us, 'May the good God look after you.'

CHAPTER ELEVEN

Anjou

During the first part of our continental ride the weather was hot and sunny. The rain and storms began in Touraine. In Maine-et-Loire it was cold and after having penetrated the valley of the Loire and crossed the river we ran into fog. Everywhere were signs of the approach of a very severe winter. In the French newspapers I read of soldiers being cut off by deep snow in the Pyrénées. My equipment – double waterproof sheets sewn together up the sides, my thick woollen blanket, my balaclava helmet, my sheepskin coat, thick woollen underwear and socks should be sufficient as I have slept in England in twelve degrees of frost. Trigger was already growing his winter coat. In winter his hair overlaps his girth and I can curl it round my fingers. My waterproof sheets can quickly contain everything in emergency, they roll up in rain in a few seconds. Sometimes I have to lie down or get up in the rain. Snow? We had slept in snow in England and been no worse for it. We were riding south but we had still a very long way to go to the Mediterranean. Gaetan, the Marquis de Meaulne, who had caught a cold while hunting and had almost lost his voice, had given me some addresses of friends and had indicated a route through Anjou. There would be no need for us to sleep in fields again just yet for a while. The first address was the château de Martreil where the comtesse de Boispéan was awaiting us, the next, Toutlemonde where the comte Yves de Saint Seine would be our host. These châteaux were old, picturesque, and very interesting. The château de Landeronde with its conical topped towers has its own chapel – a separate building – where the ancestors of the marquis are buried. His great-great-great grandmother narrowly escaped the guillotine in the French revolution by hiding in a secret place in one of the towers. The château de Martreil bristles with tall pointed towers.

We crossed the Loire at Montjean and rode due south into the Vendée. There the change in the character of the countryside is very marked. A greyness had now crept into the scene. Gone were the gay umbrellas and brightly painted *volets,* the buildings were drab, dun, without shutters, the stone a sort of pepper-and-salt colour, the doors and window frames were painted in dull tones. There were fewer cafés. Even the châteaux, like the farms, appeared somewhat seedy and pinched. When I mentioned this impression to the count Yves de Saint Seine he said that it had always been so south of the Loire, in history. The châteaux north of the Loire were nearer to the court. The count, a very charming man, was living alone at Toutlemonde, while his wife was in Paris. As an ex-cavalryman, he saw first to my horse on my arrival. He is fond of riding and hunting, and also of painting, but he took me out into a field to see his five horses before we went to look at his paintings. He had just bought another horse – 'My cousin says I'm going to ruin myself buying horses,' he laughed. When he was showing me several portraits he was painting of a girl friend he was more composed, and he asked me my opinion of certain effects he was trying to get in the expression of her face. Relaxed, and laughing again he asked me how I had got on with the countess Boispéan. Then he told me how he was manufacturing and bottling 'Yaourt' from the milk of his cattle, and let me taste from several jars with different flavours – raspberry, and so on. 'Plenty of money is coming in but my accountants say that I am not making any profit.' He could not have dinner with me that night and he apologised for the servant who had to look after me – 'she is very efficient but rather simple-minded' – but next day, Sunday, he cooked our lunch himself in the kitchen. 'I'll make you a Chateaubriand,' he said, carving a thick steak. He joked about women. 'They run after me more now that I have a touch of grey hair.'

The next stop for Trigger and me was in the open again,

roughing it. It was too far in one day to reach the château de Clisson near Bismé where we were to be guests of Monsieur and Madame de Beauregard. This château is comparatively new, the old one having been burned down in the French revolution, but the ancient stables are still there, and there Trigger slept again on straw with plenty of oats and hay. I was shown round the pigeon lofts, the kennels, and the chapel, and a secret passage.

The baron and baroness Davillier were our next hosts in a moated castle with a drawbridge, the château le Theil, but I insisted now on sleeping with my horse again. We had still a long way to go and Trigger rested much better when I was with him. Actually these invitations to luxury quarters in French castles were becoming rather embarrassing to me. It was interesting to me as an Englishman and an ex-weaver to enter the homes of all classes of French people but I hated to be separated from Trigger even for a few hours.

The market at Parthenay – the biggest agricultural market in western France – was being held when we got there. It was difficult to get through the crowded streets of this old fortified town with its ancient gateways. The architecture everywhere was changing now and the roofs were not so steep. After several nights in the open we arrived at Poitiers. The comte de Saint Seine, cousin of Yves de Saint Seine, welcomed us at his château.

South of Poitiers, avoiding the traffic of the *grande route,* we rode through Civray, Ruffec and Mansle, and on the way were given hospitality by the count and countess de la Débutrie at their château near Marney. We also stopped a night at the Abbaye de la Reau, guests of Antoine de Frémond de la Merveillère who lives with his two daughters in the spacious old hall of a monastery surrounded by ruins. There I dined on venison in an enormous stone-flagged vaulted hall with an open fireplace burning logs.

Trigger was shod again at Condac and we rode under grey skies through the country of the Maquis, desolate stretches of woods and heath, very sparsely populated. It was here that so many desperate combats were fought by the Resistance men in 1944. At the Abbaye de la Reau, arriving as I did on horseback and dining with the two young women and their father secluded in that stone-flagged, vaulted halls I had felt to be in the Middle Ages. Now I felt to be living through more recent history. Actually my reception at one place was almost clandestine. I, an Englishman, had come to a small town. A stranger met me and handed me a note which said in French, 'Go to M. Troune on the square. He will direct you where to go.' In the square, M. Troune was waiting for me. Without a word he walked in front making a sign for me to follow, and led me to a small hospital clinic which is run by a doctor who was leader of the underground resistance in the war. There, in a snug little room behind the operating theatre, I found a group of four men and the doctor waiting for me. We had drinks and a chat. All this happened without any previous notice to me. I did not know who they were or how they knew who I was and that I was coming, and I would not have known that the doctor was an ex-leader of the Resistance if I had not caught sight of a commemorative plaque on the doorway of the clinic.

In Charente the hospitable farmers gave me drinks of wine of the harvest, home-made cognac, 'calvados of the house.' The weather was very cold. I often warmed my hands in Trigger's mane or under the saddle. We found an opening to a little field and slept again *à la belle étoile,* as the French say, when you sleep under the stars. Then, after sunless days, wonder of wonder the sun and a running brook where Trigger could refresh his tired feet. Then another wonder – two farriers within a mile of each other! Then came the cold mist again and the sun forsook us. But despite the greyness of the sky and the misty horizon the trees were like lanterns with their fiery red and gold leaves shedding pools of golden light on the grass. In the woods the silence was broken only by Trigger's footsteps, the patter of falling acorns, the cawing of distant crows, and perhaps the tinkle of the silver top of my crop catching my monocle.

Near Brantôme we came across a sign on the road: 'Silence. This is the Garden of the Martyrs.' On the right of the road a sloping lawn led up to a bank of grass-covered earth and a monument. Twenty-six patriots from Limoges were shot here during the resistance.

A boy on a bicycle followed us early that morning. He rode alongside for a while then said shyly in French, 'My mother woke me. She said, "that is the Englishman who has passed".' He was quiet for a while then even more shyly he began to speak to me in English. He said that it was the first time in his life that he had spoken to an Englishman. At that spot we were certainly well off the beaten track of tourists. And yet, in that lonely part of France, so silent and almost deserted, there seemed to be an intimate and mystical affinity with England.

An escort of honour came out of Bergerac to meet me. Trigger saw them first – six cavaliers. He quickened his pace although he was very tired. After much hand-shaking and salutation the three men and three young women turned and rode with me. The clatter of hoofs and the proximity of other horses was a joy for Trigger. Although he was loaded with saddlebags and they were not, he kept up with them in high spirits. At a crossroad in the lonely tract of wood and heath we passed a post on which was a stainless steel plaque: '*EN CES LIEUX fut effectué le premier parachutage mixte de personnel et d'armes réalisé en France par le War Office britannique . . .*' Then followed the names of those who had organised the reception on the ground and those who came. Here again nothing was said to me on the subject by my companions but there was that curious wordless understanding. As we neared Bergerac we took a short cut across a field. One of the riders, a girl, broke into a gallop. Trigger, although tired – we had come farther than usual that day – at once broke into a gallop too, to the cheers of the men. How can anyone wonder at my sleeping with such a horse to please him, and to let him rest more contentedly? He had already come more than half-way across France. Sometimes I had walked a mile or two but most of the time I had ridden. He had come on foot all the way. And yet I was footsore, my buttons off, holes in my jacket, boot heels down, broken finger nails with blood spots, but after a hot bath and a hot meal I was bursting with health. Trigger was given shelter and straw at the riding school and I joined him on the straw.

As an Englishman I envy the French for the way they have organised horse riding on a national scale. At Angers on the Loire the Cercle Hippique gave Trigger oats and hay, and Commander Bercheny – *ancien écuyer du Cadre Noir* – threw a dinner party for me. A merry lot they were, talking, laughing, joking over venison and wine. At Angoulême in Charente and at Périgueux in Dordogne the horse clubs gave me a jolly welcome with dinner, wine, and song. One song – toasting with wine:

> *A nos femmes*
> *A nos chevaux*
> *A bas St. Georges!*
> *A ceux qui les montent*
> *Vive la cavalerie!*

From Bergerac we crossed the river Dordogne. A shoemaker – a Spaniard, a veteran of the Spanish civil war – repaired my boot heels while I waited and would not accept any money. With Trigger curry-combed and brushed, his feet anointed, with plenty of oats in the bag in front of my saddle, my boots repaired, our morale was high. Trigger had had seventeen hours of rest, I had had two hot baths, bought new razor blades, fresh batteries for my torch, and the sun had come out at last. I talked to a farmer who had just migrated to Lot et Garonne from Normandie, moving all his live and dead stock from the north by rail. He looked at the sun and the land around him and said: *'C'est le commencement du Midi.'* But it was not, for me and Trigger. The cold set in again and we still had a long way to go.

Near Castillonnes we slept in a field on a high hill in wet grass. It was bitterly cold. Hoar frost in the night turned the field all white. Trigger slept by my side but in the morning I could not catch him, he was so high spirited and out for fun. I suspect also that he had had enough of the road. 'All right,' I shouted to him. 'Good-bye! I'll go along without you.' He watched me, he would not believe me at first, but when he saw me turn the corner and go out of sight along the road he neighed piteously and soon appeared on the road looking for me. Before we got to Villeneuve-sur-Lot I tied Trigger up to the railings of a schoolyard opposite a bar where I went for a drink. As it happened school was just over for the day and soon Trigger was surrounded by children. Some ventured into the bar to look for me. 'The blacksmith has a stable,' said a girl and although I told her that we did not want a stable she ran to ask if Trigger could stay there. 'He gives permission!' she cried, running back, hopping and dancing with excitement. Just then her mother came and boxed her ears. 'Catherine has not done her homework,' she said. Meanwhile a boy had brought Trigger a secret supply of oats. He was whispering. I went across and listened to him. I heard him address each of the other boys in turn by name and swear them to secrecy about where he had got the oats.

Trigger and I moved on. Miles and miles of hard road, hard as a tombstone, now passed under Trigger's feet. On each side were gentle hills, all cultivated, mostly vineyards down to the edge of the road, and not an inch left. No footpath or grass verge but a deep channel ran beside us. It was impossible to get off the road. Imagine a whole day like this with the added anxiety about where we might sleep that night. It became monotonous, demoralising, I longed for the relief of something dramatic, a village or even a house. Suddenly Trigger shied and snorted. He began to trot in a prancing, bouncing way, his nostrils wide, his head high. A pair of oxen with a plough was moving slowly in a vineyard a fair distance away. When we had trotted out of sight of them – which took a while as they were moving in our direction slowly and it was this ominous slowness that seemed to frighten Trigger – I felt worried. If Trigger was going to be scared of long horned oxen it was going to be a nuisance.

Through Villeneuve we went, then down the hill into Agen and alongside the river Garonne. From Agen we took to the canal bank. The soft ground on the tow-path and the fringe of grass was welcome but there was no sun. We slept by the canal one night – a damp, chilly night, I could feel the cold through my blanket, but next day I felt so warm walking by the side of Trigger that I drew my woollen pull-over over my head and fastened it under the flap of my saddlebag. A mile or so farther on I felt for my monocle to read a sign and it had gone. When snatching my pullover off I had forgotten the cord and my monocle had fallen on the tow-path. Although there did not seem to be much chance of finding it now. I decided to have a try. I tethered Trigger where he could eat grass and returned along the tow-path. Trigger watched me anxiously and when I disappeared round a bend he gave vent to a heart-rending neigh. Luckily I found my monocle. I caught the gleam of it in the grass. Trigger chuckled and took my sleeve in his teeth, relieved and happy that I had not forsaken him after all.

Next day the fog was so thick that we had to halt and stay in a wood nearly all day for safety. There was no wind and the air was icy cold and raw. Puffs of vapour came from Trigger's nostrils. We were able to continue later in the day by creeping cautiously along the edge of the main road. At Castelsarrasin we halted again, for the night this time. Trigger needed shoeing again and I found a farrier. I was invited to supper by a horse dealer who also provided a stable for Trigger. I felt uncomfortable when I discovered that he was not only a dealer but also a horse-butcher, and my uneasiness was not dispelled when he remarked casually as I ate my grilled steak, 'That's horse.'

On the following day in Castelsarrasin, newly shod, Trigger had a new adventure. The horse butcher took us to visit a friend of his, a veterinary doctor, who kept a 'zoo'. In fields on the outskirt of the town he had some very small Shetland ponies which he bred for a circus. Trigger was delighted to meet them but he had a shock when he caught sight of some dromedaries. He was terrified. He snorted, blew noisily with his head up, reared and pretended to be fierce but he was shaking with fright and it was all that I could do to stop him from bolting. The lovely ponies notwithstanding, Trigger was relieved to get away from Castelsarrasin along the road to Toulouse.

No sun, no sun, no sun, day after day, it was so depressing, so monotonous, and so surprising in the south of France. In Toulouse Trigger tasted with relish the sugar 'violets'. Angers is famous for its invention of the liqueur *cointreau*, Périgueux for its mushrooms, Agen for its prunes, and everybody has heard of the violets of Toulouse. We were welcomed by the Centre Hippique of Toulouse and I bought leather in the town and repaired my saddlebags and harness.

Our next night in the open brought about a curious experience. I had arrived at a small village, my torch batteries had given out, it was dark and too late to trouble a farmer about a field so we were preparing to sleep in the corner of a field by the road when I heard footsteps and a voice in the mist. A farm labourer was passing on a path. 'You are going to sleep there with a horse?' he asked. When I said 'yes,' he said, 'There's an empty building there, you could sleep in there.' 'Does it belong to you?' I asked. 'No, it belongs to nobody. And I can bring you some straw.' I opened the door and looked inside. It was a tall building but not wide or long, there was just nice room for a horse. Presently the man returned with a bale of straw on a fork over his shoulder. When he had gone I spread the straw but Trigger refused to go in. Obstinately he dug his heels in and stubbornly resisted all my efforts to get him in. Even the nosebag full of oats failed to entice him through that door. We both slept outside. Next morning when daylight came I was able to read a notice on the door:

'Défense d'entrer. Danger de mort.

It was an abandoned electricity transforming station.

When I told about this to a journalist who met me on the road to Carcassonne the headline of his story in next day's newspaper ran: *William Holt, l'Anglais qui fait le tour d'Europe sur un cheval lisant le français, vient d'arriver à Carcassonne.*

CHAPTER TWELVE

Continentitis

We were now skirting the southern fringe of the great Central Plateau at its nearest point to the Pyrénées, riding through the narrow gap of Carcassonne, the old way to Aquitaine. No wonder that this point was chosen for the building of a fortress which has been strengthened time after time all through the centuries of history by Romans, Visigoths, Franks, Moors, feudal lords, seneschals, and Kings of France. And what a fortress! It is the most impressive I have ever seen. The first time I saw it was from the train in the setting sun on my way to the Spanish Civil War. Now I was approaching slowly on horseback after many days passing through featureless country. It was dramatic. To see the walled city of Carcassonne from a distance on its hill was like being suddenly carried on a magic carpet into the Middle Ages or even into fairy-tale land. The fortress is even more astonishing when you get to it and see the height and thickness of its walls and its prodigious extent, its numerous towers of different architecture, all designed for military defence in the different periods of history. Its shape is at once severely realistic and romantic, realistic in its ominous weight and significance, its immense size and incredible extent, romantic in its heavy grace which evokes thoughts of the pomp and magnificence of the chivalry of the past. It took me the best part of a day to ride round the outer walls of the city. The footsteps of my horse awakened echoes in the ramparts and perhaps ghosts from the days when the vicomtesse Adélaïde held her courts of love, surrounded by troubadours.

Down in La Ville Basse it was market day and Trigger was more interested in present-day life, particularly in the

fruit and vegetable market. While my thoughts were still
in the past a messenger arrived from the local riding club.
He had been sent to find me and invite me to visit the club.
As Trigger and I approached the *manège* in the chemin de
Serres members of the riding school, men and women, began
to sing 'It's a long way to Tipperary' and rounded it off with
'God save the Queen'.

Along the road, hospitality was being offered to me by
unexpected circles. On the way from Castelnaundary I was
guest at a girls' school – an unusual place for a man with a
horse to stay the night. It was a boarding school on an
agricultural estate with a barn and stables. After meeting
the students I dined with the teachers in a hall with the girls
looking down at me from an inside window like women in
a harem. After dinner all the girls were permitted to visit
Trigger in the stable. Next morning the girls had prepared
a surprise for us. They accompanied us down the long drive
to the main road, supervised by the schoolmistress, and
suddenly burst into a song they had written and composed
during the night: 'Good-bye Sir William and Trigger, Good
luck and fortune on the way, happy adventures...' At
Lézigan, after leaving Carcassonne, I was met on the road
by a young man who invited me to the *Maison des Jeunes
et de la Culture* for dinner and afterwards to the farm of
the domaine de l'Etang.

It was foggy again the morning we left the farm, the sun
a pill in the sky a hand's breadth up, but soon the fog cleared
and there came the first real signs of the south. It was the
impact of the Midi on the weather, on the sky, the clouds
were torn, there was more light and shade, the clouds had
shape, in the round, with shades of blue behind. The softness,
the gentleness of these blues was lovely. Lovely it was to see
something happening in the sky. Oh! this light on Trigger,
and the new scene, the purple distances, trees the colour of
grapes, the gentle contours of hills, softness everywhere.
The vines and bare rocks were lit by the sun, gone was the
leaden light, the shapeless slate grey of an overcast sky. The
shapes of the cypress trees were classical and there were sunlit patches of cream earth. But while my head was in the

clouds, Trigger was startled by a herd of goats. Later we passed a shepherd leaning on his crook, watching a flock of sheep.

But Trigger was tired, and so was I. An ache in my right arm was now so bad that I could hardly lift my arm. Because my horse was tired I walked a lot, holding the bridle and trying to help Trigger along. My plan now was to reach the coast as soon as possible and give Trigger a long rest. An old friend of mine, the French painter, François Desnoyer, whom I had first met in London in 1946, had invited me to visit him in Sète, but I could not explain this to Trigger. He could not see this on a map as I could. All he could see was the eternal road. So, as usual, although the man was tired, the horse was more tired than the man. At first I thought that the ache in my arm and shoulder was rheumatism – I had been warned many a time that there was a danger of this if I slept in fields in the rain. When I told my old farrier in England that I had never suffered from this complaint, he said, 'You bloody well wait!' I discovered that the ache in my arm was not rheumatism. It was with holding the bridle when walking on the left side of Trigger on the right of the road in France when he began to show signs of fatigue. As soon as I tried walking on the other side of him and holding the bridle with my left hand when there was no traffic my right arm began to ease.

A new and curious mental malady had caught hold of me. I was impatient now to catch a glimpse of the Mediterranean. Each time we topped a rise I looked eagerly ahead hoping to see it although I knew that it was still a long way off. Sometimes I climbed to the top of a hill to look but there was still no sea. This obsession grew and grew. Soldiers in the concrete corridors and deep underground passages of the Maginot Line in 1940 suffered from a malady of the mind called 'concretitis'. We had been travelling hundreds of miles over land across France. From Boulogne, as the crow flies the distance was nearly five hundred miles, but we had zigzagged all over the middle of France, travelling at least three times that distance. Land, land, as an islander I was overwhelmingly conscious of the mass of land of the continent. Travelling slowly on horseback is different from travelling by car. I had seen every inch of ground in front of us all the way. And now all that mass of land was in my consciousness, weighing me down, and I was tired. I was suffering from 'continentitis'.   ╱

Trigger seemed to sense my feelings and sometimes hurried despite his own fatigue. But his nose touched my toe more often now and I dismounted and walked more miles by his side.

I had read of Peshkov. In 1889, Dmitry Nikolaevitch Peshkov, a young Amur cossack lieutenant began a ride in November from Blagoveshchensk to St Petersburg. He rode across Russia in the depth of winter, a distance of nearly 5,500 miles. He was riding a Siberian pony called Seriy and he did it in 194 days. Now that I was feeling tired I thought of Peshkov and I talked to Trigger of Seriy.

A pleasant break came for us as we descended the hilly road towards Narbonne. A married couple from Catalonia had taken over a roadside restaurant. It was called 'La Caille qui chante'. They were celebrating, and the restaurant was crowded with guests. Trigger caused quite a sensation and to their surprise when in a jocular way they invited him in he walked calmly in with me up to the bar. He would drink only water but they lavished titbits on him. The *patron* and *patronne* were delighted to find that I spoke Spanish. They regaled me with wine and were ravished when I insisted on drinking it *au pourrou* as they do in Catalonia, that is I squirted it down my throat from a flask with a spout.

That night, near Narbonne, when we lay down to sleep, Trigger put his head on my chest and sighed. Cold, rain, fog, and the many hardships of the road had been shared and now fatigue had brought us even closer to each other.

It was hard to believe, but we travelled two days along the coast road eastwards in the direction of Sète and still had no glimpse of the longed-for sea. According to the map it was quite near, only a few miles away, but it was hidden from us by low dunes. We trudged on to the town of Béziers, the knolls and low hillocks and dunes on our right, the black mountains and the Cevennes in the distance on our left, then turned south-east. Surely now we would come to the sea, but not a peep of that blue line ever came. We followed the road by the canal du Midi that runs to Sète and slept a night near Agde. This is a port and ships were tied up a few yards from where we slept, but the water was only an inlet from the sea, and the sea itself was still hidden from us by low hills though now only two miles away. While Trigger was eating his oats I walked quickly up a steep street in Agde to the houses on the ridge but blast it all! I could not see the Mediterranean. Some mounds were in the way.

Trigger was puzzled now at my behaviour. I was land-sick, more than impatient, angry. He was enjoying the sun-shine and the luscious grass that grew on the roadside everywhere. Sometimes he took hold of my sleeve and held it in his teeth gently. Instead of butting me now he rubbed against me almost tenderly. People were amused to see him take a sweet from my mouth and they were astonished – and I was at first – when I said to him, 'Kiss me', and he did! Instead of playfully trying to bite me he put his soft lips to mine. We were able to get some oats in Agde and we left the hilly streets behind.

All of a sudden as we topped a low hill there was the sea, a quarter of a mile away. The Mediterranean. I was calm, almost in prayer, calm like the sea with its vast level horizon. I was looking at the Gulf of Lions. This was the edge of the land mass. We had come all the way across the continent. When we reached the beach I took everything off. We both plunged into the sea.

A few boats were high and dry, boats shaped like those in pictures painted by Van Gogh. The lonely beach was steep and deep, with blue shingle. When we came out the wind was cold but we were warm and happy. Trigger pawed and snorted. The salt water had refreshed his tired, sore feet. Feet that had walked all the way across the Continent from the English Channel at Boulogne. And now in the far distance I could see Sète. Dots of white houses covering a hill. And a straight road, miles and miles, leading to it.

Rest. We were going to rest there. Trigger was going to
have weeks of rest. I had plenty of time to adjust myself to
this new phase in our long journey. The road ran straight
ahead to vanishing point with the sea on one side and a great
lake on the other but Sète, although it did not change or
grow bigger as we plodded on, did not vanish. It was there
ahead all day long.

François Desnoyer with his wife Suza came out to meet
me in their car. I had dropped him a postcard from Narbonne. He had not expected that we would be already so
near to Sète as I had told him that Trigger was very tired.
He got out of his car, a tall, upright figure, vigorous despite
his years, wrapped in a thick double-breasted coat, and wearing a tweed cap and dark glasses. 'Desnoyer,' he said, intro-
ducing himself – we had not seen each other for nearly
twenty years.

He wanted to get me a motor horse-box – he said he had
arranged for this – but I patted Trigger and said, 'No.' We
would finish it now on foot.

After spending a whole day with Sète in sight we at last
arrived at the Corniche. Desnoyer had gone ahead to arrange
for a meal and accommodation: first a drink at the first café
bar, then food and rest at a small hotel and restaurant called
'Chez Atilla', on the Corniche overlooking the sea, where he
and Suza had lunched and dined every day for nearly twenty
years. A place had been found for Trigger in a kind of
grass-grown garden where he could see me and where in
one corner was a snug dry shed with straw for him. 'You
must stay in Sète a long time, resting,' said Desnoyer. Soon,
Trigger and I were asleep, he on his straw, I for the first time
for many weeks in bed. It was rather like being at home at
Kilnhurst again and Trigger seemed to know it. He was
content on his straw with me only a few yards away in this
lovely little white hotel restaurant with its vines creeping
all over it and its chairs and tables outside, and the two
sisters – Germaine and Raymonde – who had received Trigger
with so much love, petting him and patting him. He settled
down on his straw at once, quite at home 'Chez Atilla'. But
for the first night for many months he was alone.

Next day I was more moved in meeting Trigger than I had ever been since I first met him in the shafts of that rag-and-bone cart. That morning I knew that he was tired with the long journey and his feet were sore, but *he danced on his sore feet with joy to see me.* I wept.

Never have I known such pure love.

Hospitable hosts in France probably thought that I was a mad Englishman when I preferred to sleep with my horse on the grass outside. Trigger searches for my biscuits while I breakfast inside the château as guest of the vicomte de Hardivilliers near Beauvais.

Washing day by the river Brenne, France. Trigger grazes while I paint and my linen dries.

Photo: A. Violle

Trigger greets Shetland ponies at Castelsarrasin, France.

CHAPTER THIRTEEN

The Camargue

The next stage in our long ride through Europe was across the wide delta of the Rhône, miles and miles of flat country, an extensive marshland called the Camargue, where wild horses roam. We were moving towards Marseilles and the French Riviera hoping to find a climate less cold. A powerful mistral was blowing.

Trigger was thoroughly rested. A fortnight with no journeys except down to the sea each day to bathe. No saddle, no saddlebags – I rode him bareback into the sea, wearing my swimming costume – and I had taken his shoes off to ease his feet. In Sète, although there was ice each morning on the pools of fresh water and it was December, we swam together in the sea. The wind was cold but the sun shone in a cloudless sky and the colours of the landscape were brilliant. A dog made friends with Trigger, following him everywhere, and sleeping with him at night. I spent many happy hours with the Desnoyers at their home, in the garden or in his studio watching François paint, or pulling out the drawers of the large cabinet containing Suza's beautiful collection of shells.

Trigger had been newly shod at Frontignan. Raymonde had insisted on paying for the shoes: 'I will pay for them and they must be the very best obtainable.' And now Trigger was excited to be off again, prancing and bucking, and giving his little snorts, 'Hurrrh! Hurrrrh!'

After Frontignan we were advised to take the 'coast road', but 'road' it was not. It was a pebbled beach – very big pebbles, boulders most of them, and steep, and the tide came high up and the sea was rough. It was very difficult for Trigger's feet. When I dismounted walking was awkward.

The clouds had returned and the beach was hazy with spray and flying spume from the sea. The tower of Palavas a long way ahead disappeared from time to time in the mist and spray. By the time we reached there it was dark. I had been told of a riding school at Domaine de St Albert but no one was there so we slept in the open. Next day we reached the Camargue.

Trigger was the first to see the wild horses. About forty or fifty of them were standing close together some distance away looking at Trigger. They were white like Trigger but not as high by a hand's breadth. Trigger neighed loudly and stopped, astonished. Then he began to snort and prance, his head high. The wild horses made no sound. At first they made no move, then they galloped south, wheeled, disappeared behind some bushes, then reappeared moving at speed north. I was walking at the time. It was difficult to hold Trigger. He tugged at the bridle with all his might, almost lifting me off my feet. The dread that he might bolt made me sweat. There were stretches of water and dangerous swamps everywhere. If he got near to the wild horses, although he himself is not vicious, a stallion might kick him to death.

The flat wastes interspersed by water were unfenced. Blond flowering reeds with feathery heads grew fifteen feet high. After our meeting with the wild horses we came across a herd of wild bulls. These were black. They took little notice of Trigger. We travelled along miles of deserted road then came to a village near the sea among sand dunes. Sand had drifted up the doorways of the houses. The village looked almost as deserted as the road. Two men on horseback passed, riding with bridles without bits, just reins to a headstall, and wearing cowboy hats. It was a forlorn scene, blond sand, green sea, the painted shutters of the houses closed and sun-bleached, but not without a peculiar beauty, silent save for the sighing wind and the dull thud of waves on the sand. Trigger was thirsty and I was hungry. Luckily we found a wooden restaurant open. It was almost buried among the sand dunes. Trigger enjoyed a bucket of fresh water – the wild horses drink salt water – and while he ate his oats I

enjoyed a beefsteak and a decanter of *vin rosé*. The low
ceiling was padded with dried reeds and on the rafters were
stuffed sea-birds. The reeds in the Camargue grow as
thick and almost as tough as sugar cane, and sea-birds
abound.

How short is the daylight in December! We lay down
quite early to sleep on the sand near Grau de Roi, the sea
roaring, a lighthouse flashing. The mistral was cold. I drew my
blanket tightly around me on the cold, damp sand, and
warmed my fingers in my armpits. Trigger got up and
nibbled the spikes of grass on the dunes. After a while it
became clear to me that neither of us was going to sleep,
and at last after midnight I got up and saddled Trigger to
continue our journey in the night. Perhaps we would be
able to rest in the daytime. With my electric torch, walking
by the side of my horse, we pushed on and in the darkness
arrived at Aigues-Mortes. This place was completely dead at
that time in the night. A solitary lamp on the long massive
windowless wall of a fortress that ran alongside the road
emphasised the loneliness and emptiness of the locality. I
rested a while on a bench in the square while Trigger stole
grass from the neglected lawn. A few miles further on we
lay down just inside the entrance to a field and slept until
dawn.

Daylight revealed a bleak scene. We were lucky to have
found a dry spot. On every side were ditches, swamps, tall
reeds, rice-fields under water. A cold wind stirred among the
reeds. I would have given anything for a cup of hot tea.
Trigger was thirsty too but I dare not let him drink the water.
No houses or farms were in sight.

Riding along the narrow road we came to a bridge, a few
dimly lit cottages and a farm. On the map it was called Silver
Real, and the bridge, Pont de Silver. At the farm Trigger
got a drink of fresh water but the farmer had no oats or hay.
He had, however, a vineyard and he gave me a bottle
of Camargue wine. I had been told that the Camargue would
be good for my horse but this turned out to be pure
romance. Stagnant water on both sides of the road and the
bitter mistral blowing made the day rather wearisome.

Trigger had pulled the brass tongues of his bridle buckles through again on seeing the wild horses, my broken finger nails had torn the linings of my breeches pockets, francs and centimes were in my boots, teasels were clinging to my socks which after being sea-wet were now dry again; repairs were needed everywhere and I could not get off the road. Both of us were hungry and thirsty all that day, the end of which came with no place to sleep. Darkness made me impatient again. I had noticed that Trigger seemed less tired and travelled better in the night but I was tired and irritated, vexed because I had not laid in a stock of food. I had been surprised at not being able to buy oats and I could not carry water for my horse. In the early darkness of the long nights of winter when for safety I had to get Trigger off the road, usually it was too early for me to sleep and I spent an hour or so in a café but there were no cafés here and I could not get off the road because of the ditches. Fortunately there was no traffic on the narrow road. We kept on going. I was walking to keep warm. All at once in the darkness we came to a small bridge across the ditch. Trigger stopped of his own accord. There was a sign on a post, 'Domaine du Merle' and in French, 'Entry forbidden'. Desperate, I crossed the bridge with Trigger. We came to a lonely farm. No welcome for us here. The *patron* shook his head.

'But I must get off the road with my horse,' I protested.

The *patron* shrugged his shoulders.

'I must find a dry place to sleep,' I said.

The *patron* indicated with his hand that there was water everywhere. But at the foot of a tree was a small mound of dry earth. Here we could sleep, and I said so.

'All right,' said the *patron* and left us. I got my saddlebags off, tethered Trigger to the tree, spread out my waterproof sheets and blanket and lay down. I was just falling asleep when a young man arrived in a car. He got out and asked me angrily:

'Who has authorised you to be here?'

'The *patron*.'

He looked at Trigger and at me in his headlights. His

face was stern but his attitude softened when I explained
the situation. 'Maybe the shepherd will find room for you
in his building,' he said. 'He is coming in now with his sheep.'
The shepherd arrived with a large flock of sheep and disappeared into the darkness. Presently the shepherd came
back and showed me a big warm building.

'You can come in here with your horse,' he said, 'but you
won't get a wink of sleep. There are thousands of rats. They
even eat the lambs.' What a place! I thanked him and
returned to the tree. I preferred the mound of dry earth in
the open. Half an hour later the young man came back. An
empty room in a farm building was thrown open for me and
some straw put down. A big dog was in the room which had
a door leading into the farmhouse. 'No rats will come in
here,' he said. 'Roquet will keep them at bay.' And there
Trigger and I slept. Holes in the windows were covered with
mosquito gauze netting nailed to the frames.

Next morning as the sun was rising over the reeds we continued along the road in the direction of Arles. Canals,
ditches, flooded rice-fields extended on each side of us and
there were dead rats on the road. The mistral was still blowing, I was wearing my passe-montagne, my sheepskin coat
over my Shetland wool pullover, Trigger was warm too in
his winter coat; and we were both rested and glad to be
moving again. The few trees were bare except for the yews,
and the stunted elms almost strangled with ivy. Enormous
flocks of sheep were feeding everywhere between the
stretches of water. The tall reeds as high as the willows were
bending their feathery heads in the wind. At last we came
to a café. I gave Trigger some bread to see him as far as
Arles where we could get oats, and I drank rum and coffee
and lit a Gauloise cigarette. Finally we crossed a big bridge
over the Rhône and entered Arles.

People, streets, shops, restaurants . . . We were able to buy
oats as soon as we crossed the bridge. I tethered Trigger
to a bench in the Parking Place des Lices and let him rest
his nosebag on the seat. While he gobbled his oats I smacked

my lips and bolted down some sausage sandwiches, made from the famous *saucisson d'Arles,* washed down with the rest of my Camargue wine which was rather sour. I still had some money but I was ready to do some sketching and make some more money to buy provisions for the lonely country that lay ahead of us, flat at first then chains of mountains. Christmas was only a few days off.

With my easel and sketching pad I made a start. I was in the country that inspired many of Van Gogh's masterpieces. As I sketched I thought of that lonely artist. He died in poverty but now only millionaires can buy his pictures. But I do not believe that he lived in Arles in misery although his suicide was tragic. I have heard of a millionaire who was asked why he had given so much money for a Van Gogh painting. 'It is worth what I paid for it,' he said, 'for the joy I get in standing and looking at it.'

'Looking at it...' Think of the joy of Van Gogh. He *painted* it.

I rode with Trigger under the railway bridge, saw the canal locks and bridges, the fields, the low hills that Van Gogh painted and we rode out of Arles on the road along which he had so often walked with his easel and canvas.

We continued east about fifteen miles then turned south to Istres. A waning half moon was setting before we got there and in the darkness we found shelter and hospitality in the stables of the Club Hippique. We were among hills again, beautiful scenery, woods and lush pasture. An immense sea inlet stretched on one side with a view as far as Martigues, where we arrived next day. Then we turned east again towards the mountains of the Chaîne de l'Estaque, sleeping at night in the open again. On Christmas Eve we slept on a mountainside miles from any habitation. In Martigues where I had bought a good supply of oats and bran I had also bought some presents for Trigger and these I hid in his oats bag until Christmas morning when he was surprised and delighted to find a variety of his favourite sweets and dainties, and apples, celery, and carrots. I would have liked to mix scalded linseed with his mash but where

could I get hot water on a mountainside? I do not carry a
pan although I have sometimes lit a fire – usually to burn
litter. There is a limit to what a horse can comfortably carry.
I dined on cheese and bread and wine. It is the only time
I have ever spent Christmas alone with a horse.

On Christmas Day we rode through the highest narrow
pass of the Chaîne de l'Estaque between bare rocks, grey
and white with blue shadows. The highest summits behind
us, we descended steeply into Marseilles.

We stayed two days in Marseilles and shared a great surprise with the inhabitants – a blizzard. Snow in Marseilles!
A tempest raged with gusts of wind up to 100 kilometres an
hour, ships were in distress at sea, huge waves were pounding
the Plage des Catalans and crashing against the Corniche
sending up clouds of spray. During the worst part of the
storm Trigger and I were riding through streets which were
almost deserted; the strong mistral that preceded the snow
had not incited the Marseillais to stick their noses out of
doors, and those who did come out were muffled up. I wore
my passe-montagne well down over my ears and my monsoon
cape over my sheepskin coat. Trigger and I, coming from
England, were more used to wild weather than the Marseillais. In a restaurant on the quay I enjoyed boiling hot
Bouillabaisse.

The wind had dropped and bright sunshine greeted us on
our way out of Marseilles towards Toulon. We rode up the
long sloping road through the foothills of the high mountain
range that towers between the two ports. Gradually it became
steeper with hairpin bends up a mountainside. Looking up,
the road above seemed impossible, a mere shelf on a precipice. Trigger's feet suffered on the hairpin bends, *virages,*
as the French call them, the camber made for cars was so
steep and slippery. My own ankles suffered too as I walked
by his side. Looking down from a great height we could see
ancient mule tracks, cream snaky lines. Trigger did not
appear to be dizzy although for me the view was breath-
taking. All Marseilles and its bay was spread out like a map
below us and in the clear air I could now see the Château
d'If – romanticized by Alexandre Dumas in *The Count of*

Monte Cristo – hidden from us while in Marseilles by the tempest.

The sun was still shining on us as we climbed through the pass of the Col de Ginèsse but in the far distance behind us a bank of dark clouds loomed. The cloud bank drew nearer, a terrible mass of dark purple contrasting powerfully with the sunlit rocks around us which were the colour of icing sugar. Inwardly I felt the menace of the oncoming storm. I looked for shelter but there was none, then I remembered the cutting at the highest point and galloped back. We were just in time. The cloud bank burst. In the drenching rain I stripped Trigger and pushed all our equipment into a cleft in the rocks. The flood water came down the road over my boots and rose to the bottom of the saddlebags. Trigger pawed the stream. I made a dash across the road and put our things into a higher cleft and we stood as close as we could to the rocks. We could see only a few yards now. Trigger stood calmly with his back to the wind and rain. My passe-montagne and my cape were now soaked with the water which was running off the rocks. A car passed close by with headlights, probably not seeing Trigger. Thunder and lightning passed over us, the centre of the storm moving towards Toulon. Presently – although it seemed a long time to us – it was light again. The rain ceased and I saddled Trigger. We were now both of us thoroughly soaked. The wind was still powerful and bitterly cold, whistling discordantly among the rocks. I warmed my frozen fingers under the saddle and we set off again. Far below on the east side of the mountain range were clumps of pine but not a building of any kind was in sight. After a mile or two we rested briefly from the wind in the lee of some rocks. Soon Trigger felt the relief of pine needles under his feet and rounding a bend we came to a roadside café. Inside were two shivering gendarmes drinking grog.

It was a long slippery descent to Cassis where we slept out that night in the shelter of some rocks on a farm called *Ranch de l'Etalon* (Stallion Ranch). The owner had hardly any buildings. He had roofed over the rocks with corrugated iron where Trigger and I lay and he gave us a little straw.

Trigger and I huddled close together for warmth. In the morning icicles were hanging from the rocks around us, the wind howling along the Chemin de Carnoux.

Our luck changed when we reached the sea. A man in a car stopped and said to me in French with a provençal accent: 'Only a few kilometres along the road is an hotel, *Chez Patrice*. You will see it on the left. There is food and rest for you and your horse.' He was the proprietor of the hotel, Guy Figuires. He went on ahead of us and when we got there he put Trigger into a shanty stable with hay and oats and literally knelt before me at a log fire in the hotel. 'Now what would you like for dinner?' he asked. I left it to him, and meanwhile over the fire he made me some *crêpes flambées au rhum* – pancakes singed with rum, and coated with sugar. For dinner I was served with potage, spaghetti, côte de mouton, potatoes, salad, ice-cream and coffee, and the wine was vin rosé of Provence – 'Domaine de Gros-Pin Côte de Provence.' I ate and drank before the blazing log fire. What a contrast to the hungry days in the Camargue, the cheese and bread in the mountains of the Chaîne de l'Estaque, and the cold rain in the pass of the Col de Ginèsse. But that was how it was now, always the unexpected. I never knew what was ahead.

In the morning I was so relaxed and the coast so beautiful I began to paint. The terrace of the hotel overlooked the cliffs along the bay towards La Ciotat with a jagged headland called the 'Eagle's Beak', sticking out beyond. In the foreground were pine trees and around me lemon and cacti. In the brilliant sunshine fan-tail pigeons flitted on the terrace. Behind the flutter of wings I could hear the gentle splash of waves on the shingle at the foot of the cliff and the faint background roar of miles of beach. This was rest. The sun grew warmer as it mounted higher in the sky and it seemed to me that time did not exist until, while painting, I heard the voice of the *patron* inside, '...*faut mettre un couvert pour monsieur Holt.*' Then presently the sunshine through the dining-room window cast ruby rings on the tablecloth from the wine.

The hotel dog, a fox terrier, had grown so attached to

Trigger that he followed us when we left along the coast road. I had to ask the attendant at a petrol pump to shut him up until we were out of sight or he might have followed us to Italy. The next hearty hand-shake on the road came from an ex-captain of spahis who had spent thirty years with the bournous. Then a young woman in a car stopped and invited me to lunch at Bandol eight miles farther along the coast. After Bandol with its harbour and yachts and blue sea the coast was tranquil with little bays lined with palms. The hotels, cafés and shops were still decorated with white dots on the windows and illuminated Christmas trees. The people were now celebrating the New Year. Around the bay at Sanary as the sun was setting I received many invitations into the bars which were gay with coloured lights. The windows were scrawled with whitening: *'Bonne Année!'* It was dark on the road on the peninsula to La Seyne. Approaching Toulon I saw what looked like a bonfire and a firework display. I thought at first that it was part of the New Year celebrations but it turned out to be a factory on fire. Red, white and green balls were shooting up. It was the pyrotechnique on fire.

We stayed two days at Toulon. We found shelter at the riding school of La Gourbren. The riding mistress entertained me with caviar, champagne, turkey and olives. Here again the freak weather brought violent contrasts. A tempest with thunder and lightning began in the afternoon and a thunderbolt fell depriving Toulon of electricity for several hours. Then came a lull and sunshine. The sun was warm, almost hot. Next day violent winds returned and another storm burst. Tens of tons of pebbles and boulders were thrown on the roadway by the high sea and houses were flooded. Several boats broke away from their moorings, were dashed against the quay, and sank. Then again the wind dropped and the sun came out.

It was Saturday. We were ready to leave Toulon. The corn merchant's store was closed so I took Trigger into the fruit and vegetable market and gave him apples and as much celery as he could eat. Then we rode out of Toulon towards the high mountains of the Massif des Maures.

CHAPTER FOURTEEN

La Côte d'Azur

We were approaching the Côte d'Azur. News of our ride
had spread before us, gloved hands waved through the sunshine roofs of passing cars, the attendant of a petrol pump
called to me excitedly to say that he had just that moment
seen me on the television screen. 'I've jumped out of the
screen and I'm here,' I laughed. Descending a long winding
road we came to Le Lavandou, one of the loveliest seaside
towns I have ever seen. From then on, the road followed
the curving bays and headlands quite close to the sea. More
sun now, more light, more palms, more cacti, the colours
more brilliant, more glitter on the sea. The white houses of
the string of villages along the coast stood out like a necklace
against hills clothed with dark trees, each village with a small
bay of its own. No more desire for something missing.
Instead a sense of arrival, and yet we had not reached the
'Blue Coast'. The scent of the mimosa was overpowering.
The colours of the shutters, the *jalousies* of the white houses
were jewel-like and the turquoise sea undulated and shim-
mered like silk.

Trigger was ravished to find such fresh green luscious
grass in winter. I loitered and let him graze, wondering
whether he, like myself, was storing up memories which later
would torment him with nostalgic longing. The road
mounted and curved round low headlands, the sea below
breathing with dreamy, sleepy sighs. And now a cove, a pink
house with green shutters and an arched terrace in a net of
trembling green light from the hanging vine, and now a
house with a match-box veranda, like a clean wooden toy
to be touched for the first time. Then at a bend a grove of
giant mimosa sun-drenched, and behind them in the distance

the spires of cypress trees, bursts of green stars of cacti in the foreground, and meanwhile, as we moved, translucent leaves reaching, hanging, turning as we passed luxuriating in the light. Some of the viridian spears of giant cacti had yellow stripes, some pale green with an iridescent sheen, richly swollen with sap, erect, stiff and still, satyr-like among the trembling leaves.

Trigger's hooves clip-clopped and the fabulous panorama unrolled. We slept on the sand by the sea in the bay of Cavalaire. After the pure night frost the dawn was very red over the choppy sea throwing the long rolling waves into relief. Violet were the shadows in the furrows, red and violet was the reflection in the foam-fringed back-wash of the tide on the wet sand. Alone we were, Trigger and I, at that hour. The volume of the sound of the sea was not on the beach, it was inside us, extending to infinity; it was quiet on the beach . . . it was the sound of music. Oh! how we loved that solitude! . . .

Trigger got up to graze. Vegetation came down almost to the sea. We had all the world to ourselves. How close was that presence now. I was loath to leave that enchanted bay.

But the sun came up. The world turned. I saddled Trigger in the silken dawn colours to the sombre beat of the sea and we moved away towards the hills. The road now climbed inland to cross the peninsula to the Gulf of St Tropez. We had it to ourselves, pasture and fir woods, and Trigger had the answer to his prayer, his feet on the soft pine needles after his salt water wade. He stopped from time to time to look all around him.

Came another of those miraculous gifts from God. That marvellous hospitality that on leaving home with my paint brushes and charcoal but almost without money, I had not counted on, not expected, could not have believed to be true if someone had merely told me in words. And again I have to thank my horse for this good fortune. At the Centre Hippique des Maures, at Beauvallon near St Maxime, Trigger and I were not only given food and shelter and welcome companionship – human and equine. We were actually invited, nay entreated, to stay all winter there. Trigger, turned loose in pasture with other horses, gambolled and frolicked like a foal. We stayed there nearly a week. The warmth and sincerity of French hospitality reached their culminating point here at Beauvallon when the riding mistress as we left, with tears in her eyes said, *'Merci d'être venu ici!'* 'Thank you for coming here!' Is it possible to express more completely the sense of hospitality?

We rode through St Maxime towards St Raphaël. On the way I pondered over the experience we had had at Beauvallon. Hardship, fatigue, and hunger shared had brought Trigger and me closer and closer together. But at Beauvallon came luxury, rest, food for both of us, and Trigger ran with other horses, free. But something happened there and then that astonished even the director and the riding mistress. I was sitting on a log mending my saddle and Trigger was frisking with other horses at the far end of the field. I merely got up to fetch something from my saddlebags on the straw in the stable, but Trigger left the other horses at once and came to look for me.

On the road from Beauvallon to the mountains of Esterel, we followed a sort of corniche or shelf along the cliff with the sea breaking all the time below, the corniche curving, sometimes with the sea glittering between dark trunks of trees, sometimes an unobstructed view across the open bay towards St Raphaël. Again everywhere were the biscuit-pink or sugar-spice houses among the pines, or below us on our right, with steps down the rocks to the sea. What fairy-like residences with sea spray leaping up towards the windows! How blue the sea, how yellow the mimosa! Looking back I could see St Tropez at the foot of the low blue hills of its peninsula, peacock colours on each side of the glitter where it was hidden in the light. Ahead was St Raphaël green and cream and Indian red with blue mountains beyond and snow beyond these. At lunch-time while Trigger stood tethered to a rail looking out to sea and eating his oats I sat in a lido restaurant also looking out to sea behind glass, enjoying fried fresh sardines and wine, a dog lying in a pool of sunlight on the floor by my side. But the nights were cold. That night we slept on a slope of grass at Val d'Esquières. I awoke with flakes of ice on my sleeping sheets and there was hoar frost on the grass; Trigger was already up, rubbing himself against a tree, and neither of us was any the worse for the crisp cold air. Our next halt for the night was at Tour de Mare before climbing up to the highest pass through the mountains that now barred our way to Cannes.

Despite the lesson I had learnt in the Camargue I was caught out again in this group of mountains with little food and no water. All day long we toiled up the steep mountain sides and through the pass. We found no cafés on the road, no water. Sometimes we stopped, our mouths parched, and looked longingly down deep ravines at a stream utterly out of reach. Although our stomachs were not fed, our eyes were. The scenery was magnificent, each bend in the pass bringing sudden dramatic views of deep wooded valleys, and the snow-capped mountains behind Cannes and Nice. But our thought now was only of water. The raw sienna rocky earth on each side yielded none.

All of a sudden Trigger halted, turned and hurried to the side of the road. He saw, or rather heard it first. A tinkle of falling water. I was astonished to see a stone well, ornamented and with an inscription on it in that lonely spot.

After Trigger and I had drunk greedily I tried to read the inscription but it was dirty, weather-worn, and overgrown with moss. I scratched some of the moss away with a stone. The inscription was in French. I scraped and scoured until I could read...

> DON DE MADAME BRAYBROOKE PEASBOURNE
> ANGLETERRE SOYEZ BONS ENVERS LES ANIMAUX
> N'OUBLIEZ PAS ... ILS TRAVAILLENT POUR NOUS
> ET SOUFFRENT COMME NOUS.[1]

Who was this English lady who gave this well? When did she pass this way? It must have been a long while ago

[1] Given by Madame Braybrooke Peasbourne England. Be good to animals. Do not forget... they work for us and suffer with us.

judging from the state of the inscribed stone. Much of the surface was weathered. It had worn away but the pure water still flowed into the stone well, and then overflowed into two smaller, lower wells for dogs. God bless this woman whoever she was! God bless her soul! I knelt and cleaned the stone. Probably she passed this way in a carriage with her horses, horses thirsty like Trigger, parched with the long climb.

It was growing dark before we got through the mountains. The only building along the road came almost at the end of the day. It was a lonely inn, three hundred years old, in an isolated spot in the mountains, dark at night, surrounded by dense forest. What must it have been like in the olden days on this old road to Italy? In the eighteenth century a notorious bandit must have been in liaison with the innkeeper for I was shown a secret underground passage, an escape route which tradition says was used by the bandit when gendarmes arrived. Even today, now that a motorway has been made through another pass, this old road through the high pass is lonely, not a pleasant place to be overtaken by darkness. And there have passed this way, before us, bandits and good ladies.

It was pitch dark when we reached Mandelieu where we slept in a field on the roadside. Next day we came to Cannes. To our surprise we were caught up by the director and the riding mistress from Beauvallon in a car. They had heard that we had come through the pass. Both of them tried to persuade me to return for the winter. They offered a motor horse-box for Trigger. Regretfully I had to shake my head. 'You'll have some steep climbing to do yet before you get to Nice,' the director said. Trigger recognised and nuzzled them, and their dog in the car, recognising Trigger, wagged his tail. Trigger was patted and the riding mistress gave me a kiss and a hug.

Palm trees were now abundant and I could smell the eucalyptus. Trigger and I called on the riders and the horses at the *manège* of Le Longchamps where Trigger dined on oats and I on 'Couscous' – an Algerian dish, hot with Larissa sauce, and mighty good. Trigger waded in the sea, a groom smeared his feet with hoof ointment, and renewed the cold water bandages which I had put on to ease his tendons on the *virages* of the mountain road. The breast-collar I had made at Beauvallon to help in keeping the weight of the saddlebags well forward on the steep climbs had had a good test. At Le Longchamps I gave Trigger a day's rest.

In the port were luxury yachts all in perfect condition, bright in the light which was brighter than that of an English summer. Even Trigger purred at this sunshine, a low soft 'Hurrrh!' The brown, segmented trunks and bowls of the palms stood out against the bright luxury houses, the fronds spread under the radiance of the blue sky like supplicating hands. I guided Trigger down to the beach to wade again but we had to come out, almost blinded by the blue of the sea against the white shingle.

On the way to Nice we caught our first sight of Cap d'Antibes. We slept four nights in the open, travelling slowly to Nice, then by a freakish contrast slept in the courtyard of the Hotel des Etrangers on straw brought by the owner's son in his car from his stables on the Plaine de Var. A horse and man sleeping on straw among parked cars may have looked strange, but it was late and too far for Trigger to go to the Plaine de Var. In the morning the scent of roasting freshly-ground coffee permeated the courtyard and Trigger threw out his forelegs and got up, yawning and stretching himself as coolly as if he had been sleeping in the courtyards of luxury hotels on the Riviera all his life. He began to rub himself energetically on an iron pillar.

I patted Trigger and whispered in his ear, 'We are going out to some stables on the Plaine de Var.' As if he knew what I was saying and understood all about it he went on coolly rubbing his ear on the pillar. 'And when we get to Cap Ferrat we are going to call on Somerset Maugham, a brother Savage of mine,' I added. 'You remember that club in London, the Savage Club, where I tethered you outside?' Trigger's head nodded as he scratched his ear on the iron pillar. It almost looked as if he understood.

We stayed in Nice and at St Isadore at the foot of the Alpes Maritimes five days, then rode on to Villefranche.

There are no fields and no farms on the rocky Côte d'Azur, so to get off the road we rode down to the harbour of La Darse after dark and slept on the quay.

Next morning we rode to Cap Ferrat to visit Somerset Maugham. It was his ninety-first birthday. A group of journalists were outside the gates of the Villa Mauresque talking to Alan Searle, Maugham's secretary. Alan Searle received us with courtesy and said that Mr Maugham was having breakfast. I apologised for my badly shaven cheeks and Trigger's soiled quarters, explaining that we had slept the night on the *quai de La Darse* where there is no hot water, and we had not found a *coiffeur* open. I imagined that I saw Trigger wink as I said this. 'As for my sheepskin jacket, I'm sure that Mr Maugham will understand that for a horseman in winter it is very comfortable.' Presently we passed through the gates, which bore Mr Maugham's Moorish sign for keeping away evil spirits, and walked up the gravel drive. Some gravel had got into one of my badly worn boots. In taking it off to empty it the loose heel nearly came off. Alan Searle asked us to be patient, he was going into the house and Mr Maugham would come to the door. Trigger, who had been ogling some tufts of grass, took this opportunity to nibble some of the appetising herbage. Meanwhile the press reporters had gathered together near the door.

Somerset Maugham appeared at the door. He was wearing a long, bronze green *houppelande,* a sort of tweed cape-like cloak with sleeves, and a soft trilby hat. He looked at the crowd of waiting journalists and remarked in a petulant voice:

'Oh, it's always the same.'

But it wasn't the same. Suddenly he saw Trigger, smiled and came over to us, shook hands with me and asked about Trigger.

'I am very fond of animals,' he said. 'Always be good and kind to him.' He gently caressed Trigger's nose. 'If I had known that a horse was coming to visit me this morning I would have dressed ready to mount.' He made a faint gesture as if about to mount. Alan Searle and Margaret MacLaren, Maugham's literary agent from London, shook their heads

at me vigorously. Maugham's hearing was failing. I drew out
my hunting horn, blew a blast in his left ear and wished him:
   'Many happy returns of the day!'
   'Very neat!' said Mr Maugham with a faint smile.
   I told him that Trigger was thirteen years old and that
when I had found him he was pulling a rag-and-bone cart.
Since then we had ridden far, and Trigger had slept in the
stables of the Queen with the chargers of the household
cavalry in London. 'And now he is meeting the greatest living
English novelist of our time. It is a true fairy story for a
rag-and-bone horse.'
   'Indeed!' agreed Mr Maugham. 'Personally, I have never
slept in the stables of the Queen.'
   Everybody had jumped when I blew my hunting horn.
Trigger alone had remained impassive.
   'Do you mind if I give him some sugar?' asked Mr
Maugham. As if he felt that there was lacking around him
some old English civility, he turned and asked if someone
would fetch some sugar lumps. And he fed Trigger with
sugar.
   One of the waiting journalists wrote a footnote to his story
in the newspaper: 'In England, politeness requires that a
horse is given place before persons.'
   Mr Maugham had to cut short his reception of the journalists. The freshness of the morning air, although clear, was
bitter, and he did not want to catch a chill.

   Trigger seized the cuff of my sheepskin coat with his teeth
and we moved off down the other side of the peninsula of
Cap Ferrat. In the morning sunlight daisies were blooming
in the grass. Passing close to the mooring inlet at St Jean-
Cap-Ferrat we were waved at for the first time from a luxury
yacht, and shortly after that, while buying oats in Beaulieu,
two women came to look for me in a car and invite me to
lunch at their villa at Cap d'Ail. We had to descend a zigzag
road down the steep cliff to the villa where although it was
January we lunched in the open air drenched in sunlight on
a balcony which jutted out over the sea. Trigger meanwhile

was tethered with his oats in the sun at the foot of the cliff. The villa is really a stone castle called *Castel d'Aglio* between Cap Ferrat to the west and Cap-Martin to the east.

Without hurrying, by evening we reached Monaco. There was no place for us to sleep there, so after a brief look round we returned to the little side road that we had seen on top of the Cap d'Ail, and there we were able to sleep on a patch of grass. For two nights we used this as our base for exploring Monaco. On the third day we rode through Monte-Carlo and Beausoleil to Menton.

CHAPTER FIFTEEN

The Via Aurelia

It was in Menton that I first built Trigger a shelter. We were there for a long rest. We had crossed France and had reached the frontier. Before riding into Italy I chose Menton as the best place to stop. We had found some empty chalets close to the sea. The caretaker, Monsieur Bernard, and his wife wanted us to stay there. At the end of an outbuilding was a space for Trigger only a few feet from the chalet where I slept. It was a simple matter to roof it over with boughs resting at one end on the roof of the outbuilding and at the other end on a wall. These I covered with the waterproof sheets which I did not need while sleeping in the chalet. All I needed now for Trigger was plenty of straw, but this was a problem. There are no horses in Menton, nor are there cattle. But eventually I was able to buy some on a mountain and Monsieur Bernard transported it in his car. Trigger was happy. He could see me in my little chalet. Each morning we bathed in the sea and then rode into Menton. As we rode along the promenade we could see the coast of Italy – Ventimiglia and Bordighera, headlands jutting out into the glittering sea of the Riviera di Ponente.

How lucky we were! In mid-winter, sheltered from the north and east winds by mountains. Every morning after our bathe and ride I tethered Trigger to the promenade rail at his favourite spot where he stopped of his own accord while I painted. With his head towards the sea he dozed and dreamed, listening to the soothing sound of the breakers and the foam bubbles bursting in the warm sunshine. Sometimes I rode down the promenade to the restaurant Le Siècle where he stood by me on the sunlit terrace while I ate *pizza*. I was obliged to be on my guard and not be distracted for a moment by my map or my sketch, otherwise a moment of

inattention cost me the price of a *pizza* that Trigger licked
up with pleasure from my plate to the delighted laughter
of children.

In the evening when the sun was setting we rode in the
other direction towards the sun and Trigger grazed on a
stretch of grass where the road begins to climb Cap Martin.
We stayed in Menton until the end of February, then, with
saddlebags loaded, oats bag full, repairs done, funds repleted
by sketches and paintings sold, we rode up the steep slope
to Ponte San Luigi.

It was with very mixed feelings that I rode up to the
Italian frontier. I was sad. I had been so happy in France.
Italy could not possibly be more wonderful. But I was curious
and excited at the prospect of seeing at close quarters the
towns with such romantic names on the Italian coast which
had tantalised me each morning in the rising sun as I rode
down the promenade at Menton. I could not bear to look
back at the country I was leaving and might never see again.
Who knows? Certainly the joys, the hardships, the surprises,
the unexpected encounters could never be repeated, could
never be experienced again.

I expected to reach Ventimiglia that day. We passed
through the French control in a few minutes but at the
Italian barrier we met with a shock. I had been informed by
the Italian embassy in London that if I was in possession of
a veterinary certificate of health for Trigger signed within
twenty-four hours of reaching the frontier we could enter
Italy, and I had got this in Menton. I had also had it endorsed
by the Italian consul there. But the Italian customs officials
shook their heads, it was not enough, I must have an *Italian*
veterinary certificate, signed by an Italian vet. 'But what's
the difference?' I protested. 'My horse cannot be healthy in
French and at the same time unhealthy in Italian.' The
officials shrugged their shoulders almost up to their ears. 'All
right,' I said, not wishing to argue with them, 'I'll pay for an
Italian veterinary certificate.' The chief customs officer smiled
pleasantly as if giving me glad news:

118

'It is Saturday. The vet won't be in his office till Monday.'

'Where is the vet?'

'Ventimiglia.'

'Then I'll go and find him.'

The police barred our way. I could not go into Italy with my horse.

Meanwhile Trigger was listening to us with astonishment. He had never heard me speaking Italian before. He sensed that we were being held up and that I was growing angry but he was puzzled by this new and ridiculous situation. The official beamed affably and promised me that in any case the vet could not pass the horse without authority from the Ministry in Rome, and he assured me, nay even guaranteed that nobody would be at the Ministry until Monday.

We were on a high ledge on a cliff, a steep bare mountain on the left, the Mediterranean on the right. 'Where are we going to sleep tonight, and tomorrow night?' I wanted to know. All the officials shrugged their shoulders now. 'Very well. We'll stand here on the road forty-eight hours in protest,' I declared.

I withdrew a little way for the sake of Trigger. Darkness was falling. We stood under some rocks clear of the traffic. A young Frenchwoman came to me and said, 'I'm friendly with the guards, I'll get you through.' We returned with her to the barrier post which was raised. While arguing with the guards in the darkness we kept moving, the young woman patting and playing with Trigger, and joking with the guards. Presently she slipped round to me on the other side of Trigger. 'You're in Italy now,' she whispered. 'Beat it.' I mounted quickly and rode off quietly in the darkness while she joked with the guards. When he heard the row behind us, Trigger broke into a gallop and for a short distance we rode like Dick Turpin and Black Bess but it was no use in these days of mechanization. A police car soon caught us up. We were brought back ignominiously and pushed back into France.

The night for us was not so bad as the frontier guards might have imagined. Trigger and I had slept out hundreds of nights before. We found a small ravine and lay down but it was cold on the bare earth. A press reporter turned up on the Sunday morning when we returned to the barrier. When the customs officials saw the reporter they began to look uncomfortable. The worried chief official said to me, 'You can go to Ventimiglia *without* your horse and have a word with the veterinary officer. There is a bus due any time now.' Presently in their anxiety to pass the buck the officials offered me the use of a car and I was driven to Ventimiglia ten kilometres away. Trigger meanwhile tethered to some heavy machinery in a quarry neighed piteously as he saw me depart. The veterinary officer at Ventimiglia railway station got on the telephone with the customs post at Ponte San Luigi and finally it was arranged that I could ride Trigger to Ventimiglia under police escort and he could remain in bond at the railway station until Monday morning. This was at least some progress. I returned by bus to the road frontier post where an anxious Trigger awaited me and we rode along the coast road to Ventimiglia. Trigger was given hay and straw under the roof of the goods platform and guarded all night by two armed policemen. Next morning, but not before noon, after telephone consultation with Rome, we were free to ride on along the Via Aurelia. I had to leave a cash deposit, and a customs seal made of lead was crimped with stamping pliers and ceremoniously fixed to Trigger's mane. 'This seal must be kept on his mane until you leave Italy,' I was told. In a matter of minutes Trigger had managed to rid himself of it.

Light-hearted now, singing, I rode out of Ventimiglia, free now in Italy. I now translated Trigger's favourite song, 'There's a tavern in the town', into Italian, giving him to understand that French was no longer of any use to him and he would have to school himself in Italian :

> *C'è un caffè nel paese, nel paese*
> *Dove il mio amore si siede, si siede*
> *E beve il vino tra le risate*
> *E mai mai mai pensa a me*

'Hurrrh! Hurrrrh!' But Trigger had already learnt the Italian word for oats – *avena*.

What was that? The dreaded clink of a loose shoe. A stop at a garage to borrow a hammer and pincers – I always carry a few nails – and the job was done. Off we trotted again along the coast through Bordighera and Ospedaletti to San Remo. *'Buon giorno! Signor Holt.'* A man had drawn up in his car. He said he was manager of a big hotel in San Remo. 'Come and have lunch with me,' he said. 'I ride myself. I have a club, the Pony Club of San Remo, at Solaro.' After lunch he introduced me to a woman who was sitting next to me in the lounge, the Duchess of Montevecchio. She invited me to have dinner with her that evening and also invited me to visit her at her palace of Saladini in Fano on the Adriatic. If I had ever had any doubts as to whether Trigger and I would receive the same wonderful hospitality in Italy as we had everywhere received in France they would have been quickly dispelled. A policeman arrived smiling with a letter which should have been delivered to me at the frontier but had been misplaced. It was an invitation to dine at the restaurant Caravella in San Remo. It seems that news of my ride had appeared in Italian newspapers and had been announced on the radio even before I got to Italy, and when I picked up the Italian glossy magazine *Domenica del Corriere* I found in it a photograph of Trigger and me. As we were about to leave San Remo along the Via Aurelia I received a message that an escort of honour was riding out of Imperia to meet us. In Imperia I was made a member of honour of the *Circolo Ippico Imperiese.* Already I had been made an honorary member of the Pony Club San Remo, and for the first time Trigger himself had received a certificate of honour – *'Socio Trigger, onorario'.* In Imperia hospitality is a very old tradition. Near the *Spiaggio d'Oro* there is an ancient chapel built of 'living stone' by the Knights of Malta for the protection of pilgrims.

Riding along the old Roman road from San Remo to Imperia we were never more than a few feet from the sea. Olives and vines were being cultivated on the steep slopes but above all, flowers. The Italians call this coast Riviera dei Fiori – the coast of flowers. Carts could not get up to the terraces; mules with panniers were used by the peasants.

In Imperia Trigger was newly shod by the farrier of the riding club, and when I wanted to pay for my meals in a restaurant the owner said, 'All your meals here are paid for by the riding club.' The inhabitants welcomed me in the streets, called for me into cafés and bars, and were delighted when I made sketches of the narrow alleys and colonnaded walks which have remained unchanged through the centuries. Trigger surprised the inhabitants by walking up the stone-stepped winding causeways in streets used only by pedestrians. My sketches were hung in cafés and I was commissioned to do portraits. A saddler cut me some leather straps to repair my badly worn harness.

The coast road from Imperia runs along a corniche over the sea all the way to Genoa, nearly a hundred miles, winding round headlands, curving round bays, never more than a few feet from the waves of the Mediterranean. What a ride! It took me ten days, but what adventures on the way! I had expected to find good weather on this coast where Trigger and I slept rough in the open all the way from Imperia to Genoa, but all over Europe freak weather was making news. At one point I was warned of a *catastrofe* ahead, a 'falling mountain' blocking the Via Aurelia. At Pietra Ligure an Italian drew me a sketch on a scrap of paper showing how traffic was being diverted a detour of thirty kilometres. On the sketch at the danger point he had drawn a skull and crossbones. The storms of the phenomenally bad weather that year had disturbed the mountainside which was still falling. It was raining heavily and a gale blowing when he handed me that paper, remarking about the *brutto tempo*. Thirty kilometres detour is a long way for a horse, especially in bad weather. I kept straight on towards the falling mountain. No doubt there would be a safe mule-track over it or behind it.

It was dark when we got near the mountain. We slept on the beach. Trigger and I were lying together well clear of the highest water mark on soft sand. During the night we were suddenly wakened by the sea coming over us. I grabbed my soaked things and got Trigger up against the sea wall

but we were cut off by this phenomenally high tide. We had
descended to the beach down a sort of ramp, a sloping causeway used by the fishermen for their boats but this was some
distance away and the sea was now up to the wall. Some steep
steps were nearer but I could not get a horse up these. It
was like our adventure in the Long Tunnel of the Rochdale
Canal in England all over again, only worse. A gale was blowing in the pitch darkness and nobody was near. With rough
sea all around us in the middle of the night and the falling
mountain not far away it was a hideous moment. The mountain was invisible in the darkness and not near enough to do
us any harm but it was in my mind. Without losing any time
I hurried Trigger through the breakers, threw my bedding,
saddle and saddlebags as far as I could up the steps and made
for the stone ramp. The sea was up to Trigger's belly and up
to my waist when we got there.

Once on the road, which was protected by an iron rail, I
tethered Trigger and salvaged my things. I tried to cheer
Trigger by laughing. He stood, as usual in such perilous
situations, remarkably calm, impenetrable, showing no sign
of agitation. He had reacted quickly to the sea coming over
him but now – 'Well, we're out of danger. It's over with now.
It's just one of those things.' He appeared unconcerned, did
not even shake himself, but I was very concerned about my
wet things. The rain had stopped. I tied my cape, my blanket,
my passe-montagne to the rail and hung my saddlebags over
it to dry in the wind. Usually when my clothes have been
soaked with rain I have thrust newspapers down my breeches
and under my singlet but the Italian newspapers in the slit
pocket behind the saddlebag were soaked. They were nothing
more than wet rags.

Daylight came at last, the falling mountain loomed before
us, but I could now see a winding track that climbed up the
mountain behind the cape. Obviously this was safe enough
unless the whole darned mountain moved. Soon we were
both hot and sweating, toiling up that mountainside, but if
we could get over the top and down the other side we would
have avoided that thirty kilometres detour – a day's journey
with a horse. It was no more than a mule track and at one

point we almost lost our way. To rejoin the track which appeared to go farther inland we had to retrace our steps; no short cut was possible on that steep rocky slope. Near the summit we came to the strangest village I have ever seen. The ways through were no more than passages wide enough for a mule with panniers and even these narrow passages were roofed over at points, by the upper storeys of the stone houses. Doors led from these interior passages on each side and from one of these a sun-tanned man beckoned me in, offering me wine. I had to go forward a few yards to an inner square to avoid blocking the passage with Trigger and in doing so I passed the door of another small *albergo* where a shout of welcome came to me from within. After tethering Trigger I gladly drank wine at both places and was warmly invited to rest there for a while. Although the sun had begun to shine again, the men grumbled at the *brutto tempo* and one of them pointed in the direction of the cape and shouted *pericoloso!* I accepted a pressing invitation to stay for lunch. Trigger was munching his salty oats and I had had no breakfast. My clothes had dried on my back up the mountainside. The wine and the *pasta* tasted delicious.

Once over the mountain we joined the Via Aurelia again. Rain was now falling heavily. After replenishing Trigger's oats bag and a brief rest at a stable the *palafreniere* said to me, 'Don't go. Stay till tomorrow. *Brutto tempo!*' '*Avanti!*' I laughed, mounting with my monsoon cape collar up. Trigger bucked with joy at moving again but soon he was frightened by the ripples on the pools at the entrance to road tunnels and galleries and my cape blowing in the wind. Cape Noli was frowning behind us. Heavy motor lorries splashed by. My cape, which had dried in the wind and sun on the mountain, was now soaked again. I dismounted and put on my fireman's oilskin leggings. Water from my woollen passe-montagne was running down my neck. Each time at the end of a gallery the wind was fierce. After a few miles of this we sheltered for a while in an enormous cave and I made a mental note of it. If no better place could be found we might come back to it to sleep that night. In the shelter of a colonnaded walk at Noli we stopped again for a rest and Trigger shared warm coffee with me – he loves tea and coffee. The wind was blowing the palm trees as badly as any trees are ever blown in Yorkshire, and the Italians were struggling with their umbrellas. In the colonnaded shelter a man was telling me, 'Noli was once a republic for hundreds of years ... sent two ships to Palestine in the crusades ... Genoa came to help us against the Saracen pirates. Columbus stopped here on his way from Genoa. Dante stopped here ...'

We had to sleep on the beach again as there was no other place, but we took great care to be well out of the way of any high tide. The pebbled beach was very steep. The sea thundered all night, breakers only a few yards away down the steep shingle. The morning grey came, distant lights went out and some strange islands were now in sight. Both of us were terribly thirsty. The sea was slate grey to the horizon, then green, waves foaming under the low cloudy sky, the spray leaping twenty feet high at the side of the wet, shining road as we approached the next headland. Just round the cape a man called to us from his house up the cliff and came running down the path to invite me to a drink of wine. Before drinking I carried a large plastic bowl of water down to Trigger, the wind blowing the water down my legs, then I drank some of the wine the man himself had made from his small vineyard.

Suddenly the weather changed, the sun came out, warm, even hot. *Piano, piano!* – slowly, slowly, take it easy – the Italians say as soon as the sun comes out, and as we entered the port of Savona I agreed with them. Why hurry? *'Non abbiamo fretta,'* I said to them. 'Take it easy.' And I might have added, *'In fondo nessuno ci aspetta.'*[1] While we were basking at the foot of a sunlit wall in the harbour, Trigger eating his oats, a priest came to me. 'I am the port chaplain,' he said. 'I speak some English. I have learned without a teacher because it is needed in my work. Will you have lunch with me?'

Along the road from Savona wild flowers were blooming. Near Albisola Marina a little girl brought me a nosegay of fresh spring flowers – wild violets from the edge of the sand.

[1] Nobody is waiting for us.

I put them in Trigger's face-strap buckles. Just beyond Varazze, after wading in the sea, we slept by the roadside. Venus was very bright in the west after sunset. The southern sky was brilliant with the stars of Orion, Aldebaran above to the right. Procyon on the left, and Sirius nearer to the horizon. The Lion glittered in the east and overhead was Capella. Leaning my head back I could see Vega shining brightly near the northern skyline. Pegasus was low, almost on earth.

We were not far now from Genoa but still a long way with a horse, and traffic on the road was increasing. While I was riding next day it began to rain and the wind sprang up again. The road was wearisome now with so much passing traffic and Trigger shared my malaise in approaching a big city. Towards evening my anxiety increased, buildings along one side of the road were continuous and on the other side was the railway; the cobbled pavement of the road was worn and irregular. It was useless riding into Genoa with nowhere to sleep. The beach again was the only possible place but the railway now blocked the way. I passed a level crossing then turned back. It did not look very promising but the gates were open and I decided to take a chance. It was now dark, the road muddy. We crossed the track and found the beach only a few yards away but it was narrow and cluttered up with boats. In the distance were the lights of Genoa. Huts along the beach were in darkness. The only building with lights was a rather ramshackle *trattoria,* a workmen's eating-house. Opposite was an iron shed without walls, a small fish market. I tethered Trigger to one of the iron pillars and gave him some oats, then went into the eating-house which was dimly lit and crowded with fishermen and railway workers. The night was bitterly cold but there was a coke-stove at one end of the wooden building and I managed to squeeze myself near to this. Above the conversation I could hear the wind howling outside. A cup of coffee and some rum warmed my inside and I began to wait until Trigger and I could slip on to the beach unseen, meanwhile darning the holes which had worn in my riding breeches above the buckskin trappings. The men were noisily,

boisterously friendly, but left me alone after they had satisfied their curiosity; some played cards, but one odd little
man with a queer voice and gesticulations kept close to me,
talking with a strange accent and using one or two Russian
words. He was obviously trying to be helpful but was wearing
a cape-like coat with collar up, and his shadow kept getting
on my work. I did not want to hurt his feelings so I began
to talk to him quietly about architecture, the aesthetic
differences between pillars, Doric, Ionic, Corinthian or com-
posite. This soon bored him away. Every time I opened the
door to look at Trigger he neighed to me. I had taken off his
nosebag and he was waiting for me to join him for the night.
Some fine snow was blowing now, it was going to be a wild
night. One or two men came in rubbing their hands and
holding them over the stove but gradually the hut emptied,
the owner got ready to close. Eventually I got up and went
out, the proprietor pushed a dog out, locked the door and
turned out the lights.

Blackness and roaring sea met me now. Poor Trigger. We
went to the pebbled beach, the dog following, and lay down
between two boats. For a little while we slept but the snowstorm increased and the fine snow began to drift. I got up
and went with Trigger to shelter under the roof of the fish-
market, the dog again following. There was not much shelter
there, the wind blew the snow in. When I switched on my
torch the fine snow was flying in horizontal gusts and several
inches had settled on the concrete floor. The dog had curled
up on top of my saddlebags. I found a large empty carton
and put my saddle and saddlebags into this. My blanket I
spread over Trigger and stood with him. It was useless lying
down, the snow was turning to slush. The wind kept lifting
the blanket so I tied it round Trigger with string. The stray
dog in his wet coat was shivering inside the carton, snow
drifting up to the top. I put my head and shoulders under
the blanket, warming my hands under Trigger's legs and
waited for daylight. And so we stood for nearly eight hours.
It was the worst night of our journey.

It was hardly daylight when a woman came down to the
beach with a paper parcel. Half a dozen cats came out from

under a boat which was upside down, and I saw her feed them. I pointed to the shivering dog when she was returning. 'Cane,' she said, shaking her head sadly. I gave the dog what food I had left in my saddlebag that a dog could eat, saddled Trigger, waited until a train had passed and the gates were open, then crossed into the road and rode through the slush towards Genoa.

CHAPTER SIXTEEN

Tuscany

The day we arrived in Genoa after the worst night of our journey we struck luck again. A man in the street stopped us and told me that there were stables and a riding school on the east side of the port. When we got there Trigger was at once given food and shelter from the snow and I was given a glass of hot grog. Trigger lay down on the straw as soon as he had eaten and I was about to flop down beside him when a folding camp bed was brought out. I was too sleepy to argue that I always slept with my horse and in any case Trigger was already asleep so the bed was set up in the stable office for me. Although it was only ten o'clock in the morning I fell instantly asleep and slept eight hours. An electric heater had been placed near the bed and somebody had thrown a horse cover over me while I was sound asleep. I might have known that I should make the most of this luxury for this was the last bed of any kind that I slept in during the whole of the long ride through the European countries. From Genoa we rode down the Ligurian coast to Tuscany and all the way down the Via Aurelia to Rome in twenty-two days, and we slept each night on the roadside. Actually I can say quite honestly that I do not dislike sleeping on firm earth and in the morning I feel more rested than after sleeping in a soft bed. I have a theory – I do not know whether I am right or not – that the human anatomy was not designed for sleeping on a soft mattress. Lying on level earth our bones remain in position but the relaxed muscles and flesh are drawn restfully by gravity towards the earth, and – for me at any rate – this is a pleasant, almost voluptuous sensation. Whether on my back or on my side I feel this sinking into rest. My bones rest and my flesh rests. If I turn from my left side to my

Trigger and I guests of the famous French painter, François Desnoyer, for a fortnight's rest at Sète in the south of France.

A snowstorm in Marseilles!

On a café terrace at Bandol on the French Riviera I sketch and sell
my pictures to support Trigger and myself.

Photo: R. Gonzales

Menton. Approaching the Italian frontier after riding through France
from Boulogne.

right this delicious sinking restful feeling is doubled. I think Trigger feels this too, and enjoys the pull of gravity and the resistance of matter – especially when he rolls. The weight of his tummy and all his pliable parts is shifted about and he luxuriates in this sensual interplay of the force of gravity and matter. He would not get half the fun out of it if his bones were not rigidly held back by the earth.

Snow lay everywhere in Genoa, making the cobbles and tramlines more slippery, but it had melted and the sun was shining before we reached Rapallo. We stayed a while in Rapallo in the sunshine, mingling with the Sunday crowds, with a view of Santa Margherita across the bay. The Via Aurelia mounts a high hill from there and then descends steeply winding into Chiavari. I begged permission to sleep in a small orchard before entering this town. There was trouble at first from the barking dog. Although it was made clear to this dog that we were guests in the orchard for the night he continued to bark and the owner was afraid he would keep neighbours awake so we moved to the far end out of sight. Who said dogs were more intelligent than horses? Another difficulty at the far end of the orchard was an old deep well with a rotting fence. Afraid that Trigger might accidentally fall down the well, I extended my long nylon rope as a protective fence in addition to tethering Trigger with a new halter rope which I had bought at a ship's chandler in Genoa. My fingers were cracked with frost, the tips painful, but Trigger and I slept soundly at the foot of a fruit tree.

Riding through the long straight main street of Chiavari there was a cold wind; only the sun's rays were warm. Where does it all come from, this cold mist in the deep valleys by the sea? The sea itself as we rode southwards down the Italian coast had a brassy, metallic glitter. And there were very few wild birds. A strange coast.

We passed a funeral procession, the hearse drawn by two black horses draped down to the ground in black velvet edged with gold braid, their heads ornamented with gold medallions and black plumes. The only mourners were nuns and little girls in grey chanting Latin so probably the mourned

one was a nun. From Chiavari the Via Aurelia runs in a
straight line to Sestri Levante.

Well, Trigger by this time was a much travelled horse but
I doubt whether in all his rag-and-bone days he had ever
seen such strange looking horses as these with their legs
hidden behind black velvet drapery. Every First of May each
year I trim Trigger up with gay ribbons and shining brasses
and fix a tinkling brass bell on his head but I do not think
he would like to have his legs covered up to the ground. He
does not like being covered up in any way. I tried covering
him up once in winter as he lay in the grass but he got up
and shook the cover off. The only time he welcomed it was
during that snowstorm near Genoa when my blanket kept
both of us warm as we stood up eight hours together waiting for daylight. One wet night in a field I put newspapers
under his head but he got up straight away and lay down
in another place. His own hairy coat grows right down to
his nose and he evidently prefers the smell of wet grass to
the smell of the Daily News. Although a cold mist came in
from the sea on our way out of Chiavari Trigger was already
shedding his hairs, a sign that the weather was going to be
warm soon. The railway ran on one side of the straight road
fenced with cacti. I tried to warn Trigger not to taste the
cacti fence. I touched it to show how I got prickles in my
fingers, which was perhaps foolish. Trigger has Arab blood
and maybe his own instinct told him that cacti was not good
for him. Trigger did not like the Via Aurelia. It was hard.
But even the ground under the grass in Italy is hard. Everything seemed to be hard. Even the oats which I bought and
which were not crushed were hard. But the road was hardest
of all. It was like walking for miles over a tombstone. The
Italians say, 'Cavallo bianco porta fortuna,' – 'a white horse
brings good fortune' – which is true. But they also say,
'Cavallo bianco mai stanco' – 'a white horse is never tired'.
This is not true. If this is an Italian proverb I pity the poor
Italian white horses. You cannot carry a pack on proverbs!
Monaco nearly broke Trigger's heart. Rocks everywhere.
Not a blade of grass. And automobiles everywhere. I bet

Trigger would have given anything for a sniff of droppings from another horse instead of the stink of gasoline. Here on the side of the Via Aurelia there were rocks but there was grass too.

At the end of the straight road from Chiavari the Via Aurelia began to climb into high mountains again on the way to La Spezia. Before climbing up to the Passo del Bracco I stopped for the night for the sake of Trigger. He was glad to graze the mountain pasture and we were both tired. Next day, a little farther up the road I was sketching near a wayside inn when I received my first commission to do a cartoon for a fresco. The innkeeper had a hole in his ceiling and was going to have the ceiling replastered. I could not stay for the plastering but the innkeeper paid me for painting a suitable cartoon. Trigger meanwhile wandered in a pine wood. Still climbing after this we suddenly came on a magnificent view, a breath-taking panorama of distant snow-capped mountains, across a deep, wooded ravine. The bare branches of the trees in the foreground stood out like charcoal against the glistening white summits of the highest Apennines. We ourselves in the pass had almost reached the snowline. The air was exhilarating. In the sun in a sheltered spot I took off Trigger's harness and he rolled and grazed in mountain pasture. Daisies bloomed and pussy willows, but there was a snow-plough parked on the roadside and half an hour later in a narrow part of the pass icicles were hanging from the rocks. Trigger had a lick at the icicles. He tried to paw the snow but it was frozen too hard like foamed glass. His iron shoes rang in the pass. All the traffic on the Via Aurelia has to climb up through this pass. Heavy lorries with trailers groan up the gradients, rounding the difficult curves and go downhill with squeaking brakes. The road passes through a gallery at the summit then out into a pool of cold air and mist, the sun sinking behind. The ground beneath us was as hard as marble; some of it actually was marble. When darkness came we slept on marble. Heavy traffic passed all through the night. Dawn brought a view of the distant sea almost invisible in grey mist, but the peaks of mountains sparkled. The road descended in hairpin bends into a deep valley ringing with the noise of waters, streams which were pale green with marble dust from the quarries and tile works. The hill slopes had hardly any soil, but healthy pines grew and peasants cultivated what soil they could gather in terraces which were higher than their width. Lower down we came to grass and blackberry bushes and a stone village. Tuscan women were carrying baskets on their heads, beautiful dark-eyed women, wearing ear-rings, walking gracefully erect with shapely breasts, buttocks and legs, their eyes turned sideways towards Trigger and me. One woman had a bucket on her head from which steam was rising. I shall never forget the joy of that morning after the icy night in the Passo del Bracco when the sun got over the top of a hill. The warmth and promise of another day with my horse as companion, the blue of the sky gathering depth, a glitter on the stream, the beautiful rocks of Italian marble, lovely creams, greens, pale yellow, grey, brown, with fantastic veins, were as fresh as on the first morning of creation, but the rocks were old and thousands of horses and men had passed that way. Trigger was happily conscious of the bag of oats lying across the front of the saddle and I was thinking of coffee, Italian food and wine at the next *albergo*.

Near the foot of the mountains Trigger waded and had a long drink in a stream of clear water which joined the rushing river swollen with melted snow. At noon that day we rode into La Spezia. High over the quayside sheds towered the masts of square-rigged sailing ships and there were many sailors in the streets. In the restaurant I enjoyed squid fried in batter, with spinach and white chianti wine.

In Italy I was surprised at the harshness of the voices of the workmen. The acoustics in the bars and cafés emphasise this, the tiled walls and floors, no carpets, no curtains except those made of hanging strips of plastic. Of juke boxes there were plenty but I saw no musical instruments in Liguria or Tuscany and heard no singing.

After La Spezia we passed more marble quarries, great cliffs of marble and at one place a water-wheel was being used for grinding marble. Marble was being sawn into slabs by a continuous endless steel cable fed with carborundum powder and water-cooled.

Rain, rain, rain. It began at La Spezia and continued intermittently to Viareggio. It was very trying. When Trigger was tired I had to cover the saddle and saddlebags with a waterproof sheet and walk in my monsoon cape. There was not much rain in the night but I would rather have it then. We passed through shallow valleys among low hills then came to a plain. The sea, although not far away had an averted look, almost sulky. We passed a kilometre stone, 365 to Rome. We had come a very long way on the Via Aurelia but we still had a long way to go. We reached the worst cross-road at Viareggio, a veritable puzzle in the pouring rain. Trigger had broken his girth and the spike of the buckle was sticking into my ankle, making holes in my sock but I could not stop to mend the girth in all that rain. The traffic was now heavier, the ponderous multi-wheeled lorries with trailers splashing us. It became dangerous after dusk with the big headlights of the lorries sweeping in front and behind us. We went to sleep in a pine wood and got off again at four o'clock in the morning, the road turning inland now. For many miles we rode through dense forest, still in the rain. After the forest came flooded rice fields and a fresh wind – I had to wear my oilskin leggings. Dead tired at last and unable to cross the ditch at the side of the road I sat on a kilometre stone in the rain. Thoroughly wet now, it hardly mattered any longer how much it rained. In pasture near by a goatherdsman stood watching his goats under a large green umbrella. My cape and fireman's leggings had just about kept my pockets dry. My matches still struck so I lit a Tuscan cigar – a difficult thing to do any time. Walking forward again by the side of Trigger I began to swear aloud in English. 'This bloody rain. It's a bugger!' And Trigger gave a belly laugh as much as to say, 'Yes, it's a bugger, isn't it.'

Towards noon, casually glancing at the horizon ahead, I saw an object on the flat skyline. It was not very high but it was unmistakable – the leaning tower of Pisa.

*   *   *

We stayed a few hours in Pisa, wandering through the quiet squares and the mediaeval streets. But this chapter is about a man and a horse on their way to Rome. Trigger drank at the fountain in front of the Palazzo dei Cavalieri and as an Englishman I congratulated myself on being able to drink good wine at the equivalent of twopence-halfpenny a glass at an hour which would be after closing time in England. But the oats were not as good as I could get for Trigger in England. We took the road to Leghorn. Approaching this port the Via Aurelia brought us to the sulky sea again. It was evening when we got there. My money had got down to 600 lire. The bad weather had prevented me from sketching. I decided to sleep in some public gardens overlooking the sea but had to wait until there were not many people about. I hung around and drank some wine in a café, Trigger tethered with his oats outside, then returned to a spot I had found behind some bushes. The moon lit up our position on the grass slope towards the sea but nobody could see us from the road.

Next day it was fine and sunny. At noon I found a long unfenced field by the road, took everything off Trigger and let him loose while I mended my harness. After he had grazed I could not catch him. 'Good-bye!' I said, leaving him. He neighed and anxiously followed on the road but ran away again when I turned back. Two traffic police arrived on motor cycles and I had to explain why my horse was loose on the highway. It took the two police and ten passers-by to catch him.

Another night by the roadside and another start before daylight, and Trigger suddenly stopped. Why? I could see nothing in the moonlight. I urged him on. Was he suffering from hallucinations? A hundred yards further and he stopped dead again. I looked down. He had his foot on the bag of oats. It had come loose from the saddle, the oats had been falling out and it was now nearly empty. Trigger had been trying to tell me. 'Good Trigger!' We went back with the bag and he sniffed at a patch in the road where about four kilos of oats had fallen. I gathered them into the bag.

We passed through a village where everybody was asleep.

We were getting used to these long early morning rides without a drink but Trigger was not tantalized as I was by advertisement hoardings all along the road extolling every variety of delicious Italian drink. He was curious, of course, when he saw a glass or cup in my hand but apart from tea, coffee, milk and Coca-Cola, he rejected a share. As for food he would share or plunder anything of mine except meat and this he let drop from his mouth after eating the bread if it was in a sandwich. His big teeth made gaping inroads into my butter and cheese when my back was turned. That night I had been eating olives. He came up to me when he heard the rustle of paper where I was lying in the grass but he does not like olives.

Although my funds were low we got through another day. Breakfast for me on three raw eggs and a drink of milk from a farm did not cost much. I perforate the eggs with the blunt end of my stylo pen and suck them. Lunch on cheese and bread, dinner in a café – a dish of spaghetti. I had now spent up, but when I began to sketch, a young man commissioned a portrait and I was able to buy another drink of wine and have a few lire in my pocket for the road.

Fresh green wheat was high in the fields and fresh grass was coming up. 285 kilometres now to Rome. Riding in the sun with my sheepskin inside-out rolled on my saddle in front of me I warmed my knuckles on it. From the Ligurian coast several times I had been able to see Corsica. Now the Isle of Elba was in sight not far away. At San Vincenzo we came to the sullen sea again and then the road turned inland. We slept in the gully of a dried-up river bed and next day I saw a curious mist following the channels and ditches through fields. It was warm water. I asked a man where it came from, was there a factory near by? No, it was natural hot water coming out of the mountain, yes, all the year round. I climbed down a slope, shaved and bathed in this water from hot springs and washed some linen.

My boots by this time were quite beyond repair, the strongest boots I had ever bought, and my riding breeches were worn thin with holes coming everywhere, the canvas of my patched saddlebags was coming in holes again. Would everything last until we got to Rome? In a big city like Rome I would be able to make more money by painting and sketching. Trigger did not care about anything but I could see that he would need new shoes by the time we got to Rome.

I sniffed the fresh scent of wild flowers for the first time that year. Pale mauve flowers grew by the roadside. We passed an orchard in full bloom with a notice in Italian warning passers-by of danger of death from poison-spray. Trigger's hairs were coming off – a sure sign of warmer weather. A shimmer of green was coming over the hawthorn. Lucerne was growing ten inches high at the roadside with bluish pink flowers. Trigger bolted it down greedily and I gathered a stock of it in case the oats ran out. A kilometre stone said '200 km. to Rome'. We crossed a bridge over a swift current, the 'Torrente Sovata'. 199 kilometres to Rome. Hurray! We had knocked the '2' out of it. Blue irises were blooming at the edge of the growing corn which was like green velvet under the scattered olive trees.

The local Italian newspaper report of our arrival in Grosseto after dark read: 'Riding into Grosseto like a prince in a fairy tale in the saddle of a white horse, William Holt, an Englishman from Yorkshire, rode up to the fountain in the Rosselli Square despite a warning from the police and quite serenely let his horse drink. When a policeman ordered him away, Holt offered to the teacher of the law his two wrists and invited the policeman to arrest him and his horse and take both of them to prison. Meanwhile patient Trigger continued to drink, his eyes calmly watching, utterly indifferent to the law and the crowd of spectators. Then, quickly getting over the contretemps, the Englishman screwed in his monocle and went for a drink in La Vasca bar quite naturally offered by his fans, after which he mounted and rode away towards other new fountains on his way to the capital.'

Actually we rode back to an open space near some tall blocks of flats that I had spotted on entering Grosseto and there we slept on the meagre grass.

Next day on the road to Orbetello we passed several snakes – some of them a yard long – flattened on the road by traffic.

Above In Noli, north Italy. "Brutto tempo," but Trigger and I are used to it. *Below* Heat wave near the Colosseum. Ice cream tastes good in the hot Roman sun.

Photo: Herbert Fried

Photo: Egidio Casagrande

. Nosebag removed, Trigger dozes after his lunch of oats in
South Tyrol.

We had often seen hedgehogs flattened, and in the Camargue, rats, but this was the first time we had seen snakes. I felt natural sympathy for the snakes, having had many near shaves myself from being flattened by the excessively large heavy lorries on the Via Aurelia while walking between Trigger and the traffic. After all, the poor snakes had missed the spring after such a hard and severe winter. Riding on horseback one sees every inch of the road. Often I have dismounted to pick up a beetle in distress upside down on the road and fling it into the grass, and I once saved an innocent baby field mouse from being flattened.

Before reaching Orbetello night came, and rain. As usual, in choosing a spot to sleep on the roadside I examined every inch of the ground to see if a piece of broken glass or anything else dangerous for Trigger lay hidden. We were lucky to find some deep grass and I could feel nothing sharp. During the night Trigger got up to graze. When I flashed my torch on him I was horrified. Clinging to his flank was an enormous shiny black thing as big as a turtle. I jumped up and grabbed at it. It was sticky. Examining it closely I found that it was tar. Somebody must have poured a bucket of tar away in the grass, the grass had grown over it, and Trigger's heat had melted it. Relieved to find that it was nothing harmful I tried to scrape it off but my efforts were useless. I would have to call on a chemist. Imagine a white horse with a bucket of tar on his flank! *Catrame* ... Although I can speak Italian I had never used that word before. I had to use it now to explain my predicament, had to buy *nafta* – strange words to use for a horse. The rock-oil melted the tar, and I used a lot of old newspapers, then a rag, and finally made a bonfire of them on the roadside.

The next night we could have slept in a wood and it was Trigger who found an ideal spot, but my moral weakness for pushing on to a village landed us late after dark on a difficult part of the road with little space to lie down and Trigger very tired. We lay on grass-covered uneven ground within a few feet of the wheels of passing motor lorries. For Trigger's safety I lay between him and the road. By next morning he had worked himself into a hollow and in getting up he had

to make several attempts with the result that he sprained a
muscle in his left foreleg. My heart sank when I saw him
limping. He appeared to get over it after a few minutes
walking but it was obvious to me that he now needed
a rest. I walked with him a few miles to Montalto di Castro
and there we stayed two days. I looked at him with pity as
he stood with his left knee bent. Poor Trigger! His tendon
was swollen. I put on cold water bandages and that eased
him. We slept on soft turf in a triangular public enclosure
by an old cannon. His recuperation was astounding. The sun
was warm now and he frolicked about and snorted with
pleasure as we took to the road again, but I promised him
a long rest when we got to Rome. There was abundant
lucerne at the roadside and flowering clover. We travelled
slowly, stopping to graze whenever Trigger wanted to. He
shied when the cork shot up from a bottle of beer in my
saddlebag which had become quite warm in the hot sun.
The beautiful mauve wild flowers waved in the mild breeze.
A couple of shirts and pants washed in a stream dried in a
few minutes. We came to a stone '103 kilometres to Rome'.
Four more kilometres knocked the '1' out. Hurray! 99.
Only two digits left! At the beginning of the Via Aurelia the
figures were so astronomical that they hardly meant anything.
Now I was counting the diminishing kilometres. The swelling
of Trigger's tendon had gone down. We rested a couple of
days in ancient Tarquinia, a long cluster of houses on a low
hill, where Trigger made friends with a donkey which roamed
loose.

We descended to the Via Aurelia from Tarquinia on the
Sunday morning, church bells noisily tolling, a windmill's
sails pumping water and spinning like mad. No, I did not
charge the windmill. My quixotic sentiments were directed
against the modern motorised traffic on the road which made
such fiendish noises, the smallest monstrosities, the motorised
bicycles, making the biggest noise. Trigger, far from being a
bony Rozinante was fat and bonny, and he himself had taken
over the role of Sancho Panza, for ever extolling the merits
and virtues of food and luxuriating on clover on the banks
of rivers in the sun instead of pressing forward on a pilgrim-

age to Rome. Unlike Don Quixote I gave way to him when we reached a bridge over the fiume Miglione. Along the riverside was a grassy bank and there we rested and even slept for a while in the sun. Rome was only sixty miles away. When I awoke I found that Trigger had stolen my lunch. He was standing over me, dozing on his feet.

The sun had almost set when we drew near to Civitavecchia, its golden ball two fingers' width above the silent sea. Before entering the town we came to an extensive heath between the road and the sea, an ideal spot to pass the night. Darkness had fallen. Without my guiding him Trigger made for this heath. We went a good distance from the road and were well hidden by high clumps of broom and stunted gorse bushes. I unsaddled Trigger and spread out my things in the light of my torch. Hearing footsteps I switched my torch out and put it into my breeches pocket. A man passed us in the darkness with a dog. Although he must have seen us he did not speak. Suddenly Trigger's head went up. A horse neighed some distance away. Trigger bolted. Fearful of losing my horse in the darkness I plunged after him with my torch and caught up with him a couple of hundred yards away and grabbed the halter. We returned to what I was quite sure was the exact spot where I had left all my things but nothing was there now. Tethering Trigger to the base of a clump of thorns I searched every inch of the ground for at least a hundred yards in every direction. It was difficult with my torch which threw a shadow behind every clump of bushes but I persevered and searched for at least an hour systematically in parallel lines over a large area of the heath until my torch batteries gave out, then I had to give it up. I tried to console myself that when daylight came I would be able to solve the mystery but a growing fear tormented me. That man who passed us in the night without speaking. Could it be possible that my things had been stolen? No, I dismissed the suspicion, and decided to make the best of the situation until morning. I had taken off my coat before Trigger bolted and was in my shirt-sleeves. A cold wind was blowing. I lay down in the lee of the bushes where Trigger was tethered but Trigger remained standing. Without a blanket I was cold, and Trigger seemed to sense that something was wrong. During the night the wind increased. I got up and led Trigger to the shelter of a high wall at the west end of the heath and there we stood. I was haunted with the thought of finding myself without saddle, bridle, saddlebags and all my equipment and things, including my passport, half-way down the Italian peninsula. All that was left was Trigger's headstall and halter. Well, fortunately I had not lost Trigger, and fortunately that night it did not rain. Lighter-hearted in the morning I searched the heath. But I could not find my things . . .

Panic-stricken now I wandered up the heath towards the road and to my horror I saw on the heath near the road a gipsy caravan with a horse tethered to the wheel. It was a ramshackle caravan and a mongrel dog was lying at the foot of the steps. Was it the gipsy who passed us in the night? In any case the gipsy must have seen me from his caravan searching with my torch for my lost saddle and equipment all over the heath. Camping there he would know the heath well. Had he found my things? In which case was he honest? I approached the caravan and knocked at the door. In case he knew nothing about my things I decided at first not to mention my loss, I merely asked him if he had any fodder to sell? He stood at the door and shook his head. Behind him I could see his family sitting up in bed. I could see no sign of saddle and saddlebags. He stood taciturn without any apparent curiosity about me and my horse. I left him to continue my search and as I walked almost aimlessly towards the sea I suddenly came upon my things. They were all spread out as I had left them between some clumps of broom, the saddlebags open, the blanket partly unrolled, the bridle lying on the grass. Oh, how happy I was to see them again, my poor battered worn saddlebags, my paints and easel, my livelihood. You don't value these simple things until you have lost them. I closed my eyes and prayed.

CHAPTER SEVENTEEN

Rome

We were nearing Rome after riding the whole length of the Via Aurelia. Via Aurelia . . . how can I ever forget you, now? What a long way! What a long time! What thoughts, what dreams, living and sleeping along this road. The long straight levels, the steep climbs, the curves, the corniches, the galleries, the umbrella pines shading us from the hot sun, the snow and ice, the rain, the marble, the thundering traffic. Will Trigger ever forget those heavy lorries and trailers? Riding, they brushed my knees, walking by the side of Trigger I stepped back and squeezed against him as the big lorries approached with headlights. Great, long, twelve-wheelers, towing trailers, looming like houses, nearly running over us. The trailers have no headlights. As the shadowy lorry passes, the trailer comes afterwards with a shock in the darkness. Between the lorry and its trailer are dim lights which cast a beam of light across the road. This beam comes like a scythe in the night towards us. I have sometimes put my hands in front of my face and shut my eyes, as this scythe of light comes at speed towards us. The din of these 'heavies' will echo in my mind for ever. So many of them, and all through the night, sometimes a procession of them coming round curves, mounting gradients with groaning gears, descending hairpin bends with squeaking brakes. A nightmare of modern traffic. And yet, although we had not then left the Via Aurelia, I already felt stirring deep within me that affection, that longing that torments me now when I think of our ride. I would not have missed it for worlds. Even Trigger, now that it is over, has behind him the grand experience of travelling the way that chariots went. We were happy most of the way. Trigger knows how happy we were.

Now we were nearing Rome, the eternal city. Trigger is not interested in history although his horse ancestors helped to make it. I saw things that took my thoughts back a long way, passing through that grave, mysterious landscape. I saw the smile on the lips of a young woman in a mural at Tarquinia, an Etruscan smile from 300 B.C. When I passed a dump of crashed cars I thought of that smile. The Etruscans knew that all things in this world are subject to Time which becomes their fate.

After we had passed through Civitavecchia the weather became warmer and one night I slept uncovered. I was so tired I fell down asleep while unrolling my blanket. That was near the 35 kilometre stone. On 31st March, 1965 we halted at the 22 kilometre stone near the river Arrone. We had been on the road eight months. I wanted to do a bit of spit and polish for entry into Rome. All around us were grass-covered low hummocks of the Roman campagna. Trigger was eating his oats while I snatched a quick meal of cheese and olives and lit a Tuscan cigar. It was then that I decided to stop there all day and overnight and ride into Rome in the morning.

'ROMA.' At last the name stood before us on an iron post. A group of people was standing there at the boundary to welcome us, including a priest. It was the beginning of the most extraordinary experience of my life. For Trigger, too, it was the commencement of an adventure of extreme contrasts, the threshold of romance. When Trigger and I first met he had only one shoe. One of his shoes is now set with precious stones in an Italian palace. I knew nobody in Rome. In Paris we had a letter of introduction. Paris welcomed us. We stayed a whole week. In Rome we stayed two months. Paris held us by wonder and excitement. Rome held us with love.

Ah! When I first saw this white horse and made my wish did I really believe that it would come true? I certainly did not imagine then that I should become a vagabond with a horse in the streets of London, Paris and Rome. During the whole of my stay in Rome I slept in the open with my horse, but under what exceptional circumstances! Much of the time I slept in a Roman street on a patch of wild grass that apparently belonged to nobody, lay down with Trigger, lulled to sleep by the all-night traffic, adored by schoolboys, café kiosk-keepers, petrol pump attendants, beggars, street-sweepers. Some of the time I left a loaded table after dining with an Italian princess, waited on by a butler in white-and-gold livery wearing white gloves, to lie down with Trigger on the grass outside the palace. When I declined the kind offer of a luxurious bedroom and bathroom I was told that I was the first guest in the history of that ancient noble family to sleep with his horse under the stars.

But Trigger knows why I slept with him on our long journey. 'There is no secret so close as that between a rider and his horse.'

The Romans who met us at the boundary showed me the way into the city. Where the Via Aurelia meets the Via Gregorio VII I saw that stretch of grass behind a hoarding where we returned that night to sleep. First we made for St Peter's Square, then to the bank of the Tiber. The striking view of the Castel Sant'Angelo with its bridge seen from the left bank inspired my first picture in Rome. I rode down next day when the sun was rising and did a pen and ink sketch. The east side of the castle was flooded with light, the angels on the beautiful Ponte Sant'Angelo were dazzling white, the arches of the bridge, dating from Hadrian, cast long shadows. While I was sketching, an Italian wanted to buy the picture. He offered me 7,000 lire. 'But I haven't finished it yet,' I said, not wanting to part with it while it was still a living, pulsating piece of my heart. 'When will you have finished it? Where can I meet you?' I told him where I slept and that night he brought me 7,000 lire. Not a bad start. On riding along the bank of the bank of the river I had seen how the winged figure of a woman with arm out-stretched bearing a laurel crown appeared to be taking off in flight from the budding trees. The sun-drenched, awakening trees cast long shadows in the rising sun. I rode down next morning to do this picture which to me after our long hard winter was the very embodiment of 'Spring on the banks of the Tiber', and I was already calling it that. With a thrill I saw it again. Then suddenly in my excitement I saw in front of me on the pavement the shadow of my horse. I hesitated. Could I permit this shadow to come in? Why not! It balanced wonderfully the sweeping figure of the winged statue in the sky. I sketched the shadow there and then. I remembered what André Lhote once said to me when we were painting together in London, '*La nature peut vous donner n'importe quoi. C'est merveilleux; si vous en avez besoin vous le trouverez.*' Yes, if you have need of something, look, and you will find it! Oh, how happy I was in that spring on the banks of the Tiber.

The junction of ways where Trigger and I slept was called Circonvallazione Aurelia. On one side of us was a rather rickety café kiosk built mainly of trellis, on the other side, some distance away, was a petrol station. In the morning the sun shone through the trellis and the thin silk of parasols of women sitting with their coffee. Attendants from the petrol pump drew water for Trigger from a public water tap across the road, schoolboys got through a hole in the high netting fence to gather lucerne on building land owned by the Vatican, for Trigger to eat. At night the petrol station closed but the kiosk remained open late, illuminated by strings of coloured bulbs. Fernando Carinci, the kiosk owner, regaled me with wine and refused payment, and there was Alvaro, a young man who helped him, a girl, Antonietta, who frequented the neighbourhood, and rascally Stracchino who shaved half his moustache off to make me laugh. I sketched portraits of all these. And there was a little prostitute who when passing used to shout to me, 'Americano! Americano! I love you. Gimme mille lire!'

Trigger loved Rome because nobody turned him off the grass as they did in London. Each morning on our way down the avenue Via Gregorio VII he grazed on the wide verge between the two-ways, and he always had his drink at the stone trough by the wall of the Vatican City. There is abundant pure drinking water in Rome, and Romans, young

and old, put their mouths under the taps and fountains in
the streets.

One morning on our way down the Via Gregorio VII a
young man caught up with me in his car. He had come from
the Italian princess Angelica del Drago with an invitation
for Trigger and myself to stay with her at her palace. A
young lady called Deana Frosini would meet me on horseback and show me the way. It was a lovely ride, the trees
budding, birds singing, and Trigger was ravished by the company of another horse. The heads of six more horses craned
over the half doors of loose-boxes on our arrival. An elegant
brunette came towards me holding out her hand. 'You are
the principessa?' I asked. She nodded and I presented
Trigger to her. She made quite a fuss of him, asked me a lot
of questions about him, fed him with sugar lumps and then
asked me if I would do something for her as a favour. She
wanted me to give her one of the shoes that Trigger had
worn down the Via Aurelia. It was a small favour but I was
proud that she had asked. 'I shall send it to a jeweller,' she
said, 'and have it set with stones as an ornament here. And in
return I would like to buy Trigger a new set of shoes and we
must have the best farrier in Rome.'

That evening I dined with the princess and with the
Italian prince Giovanni, and the Bourbon prince Giovanni,
whose grandfather was king of Naples and Sicily before he
was deposed. Trigger was happy in a field of luscious grass
into which another horse had been let loose for company.
This was the beginning of a happy interlude and a rest which
lasted for many weeks. Sometimes the chauffeur drove me
into Rome, sometimes I rode Trigger. The police in Rome
would not let me set up my easel in the streets so I often
sketched in the saddle. If I returned late from Rome the
princess would tell me next day that she had left her bedroom
window wide open to listen for the footsteps of Trigger.
Although most of the conversation was in Italian, she and
her family and most of the guests that came could speak
several languages fluently. French was often used and when
a baroness came with a dachshund which had been bitten
by a viper and saved in the nick of time by a veterinary doctor

the conversation switched into German. The company was
always gay in that dining-room brilliantly lit by a glass
chandelier with blue candles. The Bourbon prince sometimes
got up in the middle of the meal to put on discs of popular
music and come across the floor dancing the Charleston
or singing 'Ma! he's making eyes at me'. When he accidentally dropped a spot of sauce from his *pasta* on the tablecloth, with a mock-surreptitious gesture he covered it with
his bread, pretending that nobody had seen it. Princess
Anna Maria leaned over and covered it with an ashtray upside down and everybody laughed. At one point while we were
smoking cigarettes I was looking for an ashtray when Princess
Angelica, who was sitting next to me, held up a small empty
plate, saying 'this will do'; everybody was talking and actually
she was saying this to somebody else who wanted some fruit.
When I knocked off my cigarette ash on to the princess's
plate there was a scream of laughter. It was the more incongruous as at the time we were talking about the Pope. After
lunch one day, Prince Giovanni fell asleep sitting on a couch
with his coffee in front of him. He had complained, 'I sleep
during the day and I cannot sleep at night. It is the end.'
He was wearing for fun a long Beatle wig. The company
entreated me to do a caricature of him. The Bourbon prince
told me that he did not ride, his hobby was cooking and he
had a wonderful kitchen in Paris. Princess Angelica asked me
if I had ever been in a city of red roofs with points, she had
had a dream about it. She was intrigued because I caught
Trigger barefoot in the dew to save wetting my shoes, and
told me that in this way I received certain vital rays and the
attraction of these rays could be increased if I stood barefoot
in the dew with a branch of fir held up in each hand. I have
never tried it. I don't know what Trigger would think of me
if he saw me doing this! She also showed me how she could
'close herself': how by folding one's arms in a certain way
one could hold off emanations and the bad influence of an
evil person. She unfolded her arms quickly with a laugh to
assure me that she did not mean that I was evil, and then
showed me how by holding the hands in a certain way she
could attract the spirit of another person. All this took place in

a lounge after meals with big windows reaching from floor
to ceiling overlooking a magnificent view of the rolling Roman
campagna and opening on a terrace. Large oil paintings hung
on the walls, one of which pictured the ship on which the
Italian Catherine sailed to marry the King of France. The
much vaunted French 'cuisine' actually came from Italy, she
claimed, taken to France by Queen Catherine; many of the
dishes and methods of cooking were introduced into Italy
by Marco Polo. Each night when I left to join Trigger in
the field, Princess Anna Maria would persuade me to have
another drink, a *sambuco* or something, and press me to take
cigarettes away with me.

We stayed in Rome until June. I managed to build up a
nice little fund by my sale of pictures, bought myself new
jodhpurs, jacket, shoes, and a panama hat. In the streets of
Rome not only the Romans but also the tourists were
interested in Trigger and I answered questions in many languages. Sometimes I would sit outside a café while Trigger
ate his oats and I would eat a *tramezzino,* a delicious Roman
sandwich, and drink a *cappuccino* – coffee with a dash of
milk in a doll's cup half full (Romans are drinking these all
day). Trigger watched me. Even when his nosebag is on, his
eyes are on me. Priests invited me to lunch, a professor from
Iceland who was recuperating in Rome after an illness invited
me to dinner, and one day in the Via Vittoria a young woman
came to pat Trigger. She had a brilliantly coloured silk scarf
over her arm, was carrying books, a beaded handbag and
flowers – Trigger tried to eat the flowers – and she was wearing fashionable white lace stockings. After a chat she gave
me her card which bore a coronet, Michelina di Vinciguerra,
a marchesa from Foggia, and invited me to have coffee with
her each morning in the Piazza Largo St Carlo. She bought
me copies of Italian songs and sang them to me in a low
contralto voice. One of Trigger's favourite spots was the
Piazza Colonna where fountains played and other horses
waited in the shafts of open carriages, tossing their nosebags.
Once, waiting for a shower of rain to stop, I passed away

the time by doing a sketch of the rain, the fountains, and the carriages with their umbrellas up. Another favourite spot of Trigger's was the grass strip by the Cavour Bridge where I turned him loose to graze while I sat outside the café opposite under the awning. There was a small advertisement in an iron frame which had iron spiral decorations. One day Trigger got his bridle hooked on a spiral. The advertisement that day had a portrait of ex-queen Soraya. I had to smile when he broke his bridle buckle tearing himself loose from Soraya! The trees were now clothed in fresh green and a carpet of daisies had risen to the sunlight before the Castel Sant'Angelo. The light in the streets was such as I had never seen before. Every object stood out, stereoscopic. I love the Roman light. Scenes beckoned to me everywhere. I was tethering Trigger one day in a narrow street before going into a *trattoria* for my own lunch when a boy parked his bicycle against the wall by the door. The shadow of the bicycle on the plaster wall was a vision of sheer beauty. The bicycle leaned carelessly against the wall, the wheels not in line, and the direction of the sunlight was oblique. I stared at the shadow in amazement. No artist could have imagined anything so surprising as the shape of this shadow. Fantastically beautiful. I forgot my lunch. A white-clad waiter stared at me from the doorway, half in light, half in shade, and there was a table of fruit and bottles of chianti just inside the doorway, again half in light, half in shade. The painted shutters of the first storey were half open, a garment hanging out of one of them to dry, and two iron lamps threw oblique shadows. The sign, 'Trattoria Genovessa', was decorated with a bunch of grapes.

What a variety of ecclesiastical costumes in the streets – nuns, priests, monks of different religious orders, robes and gowns blowing in the wind; there was always a wind while we were in Rome. I sketched these in movement, on horseback, and the picturesque carabiniere. In the streets was a nonchalant, tolerant atmosphere, traffic giving way to my horse, police often halting the traffic for us to pass. Whenever we stopped the Romans gathered round us, smiling and passing ingenuous remarks, unaffected like children, and

nobody in a hurry. Watching me sketch they would exclaim,
'*Bello, bello!*' Trigger knew his way about Rome. He could
find his way to the stretch of wild grass at the Circonvallazione Aurelia where we slept if I dropped the reins in the
evening in the middle of Rome. If I wanted to go to our other
home-from-home in Rome I had only to turn to the road
to San Cosimato or even mention it and he would find his
way to the Tenuta del Drago. Sometimes we rode up to the
Villa Borghese where Trigger could graze and roll on the
grass. When we first arrived in Rome in April the cafés, bars
and shops were stocked with sweets, chocolates, and dolls for
Easter. Italians have a sweet tooth, there are always more
sweets than savoury confections displayed in the bars.
Trigger's tooth is sweet and he enjoyed Italian sweets. As
the weeks went by both Trigger and I became more and
more settled in Rome. Rome had received us in a wonderful way. One day a man came up to me in the street and
said simply, 'Rome loves you. Don't go away.'

In May, the Princess Angelica said to me at dinner, 'The
count Pirelli invites you to the international Concorso Ippico
di Roma. He wants you to meet him at the Piazza Siena.'
This was a great day for Trigger. Hundreds of horses, including cavalry in formations with drums and music,
squadrons with white horses, squadrons with black, and
horses from all over Europe competing for prizes in racing
and jumping. I was very disappointed that no competitors
had come from England, especially when at the close there
was a salute to the flags. I fastened a little Union Jack to the
roll behind the saddle. Trigger was the only horse there from
England. He held no record for jumping or racing but I
don't believe there was a horse who could have stood up to
what he had done. He had come all the way from England
to Rome, sleeping rough through one of the worst winters
in living memory. That was a sporting achievement.

When June came we were ready to ride across Italy to the

Adriatic. The hot weather had not yet arrived and I had heard of snow in the Apennines. A French guest of the princess at dinner said that he had come through flooded roads in his car from Naples. Freak weather yet, but Trigger and I had had plenty of this. Princess Angelica wanted me to stay on in Rome and let Trigger go back by boat, 'He has come all the way to Rome. That's enough for a horse for a lifetime,' she said. I had had a vet to look at Trigger's foreleg on my arrival in Rome. He had said that it was not serious and it would do him no harm to continue after a rest. Now he was quite fit. *'Chi va piano va lontano,'*[1] I quoted. A few days before we left, Tom, one of the princess's dogs worried my new panama hat. I could hardly blame him. I was lying in the grass with Trigger when the wind caught my hat which was on the ground and blew it across the field. The temptation was too much. Next day Prince Giovanni, who had gone with Princess Angelica into Rome, rang me up to ask what size of hat I took. Later, the princess handed me another new panama, saying, 'A present from Tom with his apologies and regret.'

A champagne party was given when I saddled Trigger and said Good-bye. The princesses Angelica and Anna Maria and a dozen guests stood on the steps and toasted Trigger and me. My glass was refilled by the Bourbon Giovanni even after I had mounted, and the party waved to us until we were out of sight. I felt a little sad and Trigger stopped several times and looked back. Servants and employees of the *tenuta del Drago* waved to us and all the horses had their heads out of the loose-boxes. It was a sad moment for both of us.

We had to ride through the centre of Rome and across the Piazza del Popolo to the Via Flaminia. The people could see by my load and the bag of oats across my saddle that I was leaving. Many came to me to shake hands and to touch Trigger, and a man said, 'You are original. We love you.'

Joining the Via Flaminia, for the first time since leaving Yorkshire we rode north.

[1] He who goes slowly goes far.

CHAPTER EIGHTEEN

The Via Flaminia

The first night on the Via Flaminia we slept in deep grass, Trigger very close to me. There was a new moon. A cuckoo sang in the morning. We were on the road early, our shadows in front of us now. It was the fourth of June, Trigger's hairs were still coming off; although he knew we were travelling north, he shared my excitement in taking to the road again. The corn was ripening, on the roadside was abundant clover and lucerne, masses of red poppies exploded their powerful colour against the blond background of wheat. Haymaking had already begun. The peasants shouted to us, '*Arrivederci! Auguri!*' The road stretched out before us and in the distance was a mountain range.

For several days we followed the curving valley of the Tiber. The kilometre stones were our companions again and at regular intervals the terracotta coloured houses of the road maintenance men with the sign, 'S S Flaminia. Casa Cantoniere.' The variety of wild flowers on the roadside was capped and enhanced by the colours of the flitting butterflies, and lizards darted over hot cream-coloured soil. At night there were fireflies. I gathered some flowers and put them in Trigger's bridle behind his ears. How lovely the colours against his white hair! Blue and red, but especially pink. About thirty miles from Rome the Princess Angelica caught us up in her car and gave me a hundred bags of Twinings tea from London, and a box of sugar-lumps for Trigger. I was lying in the grass with Trigger leg-deep in straying oats with ripe ears, balls of clover dripping from his mouth, the quiet countryside made even more peaceful by the cooing of doves.

My new light summer jodhpurs were cool and I rode some-

151

times with my feet out of the stirrups; my new soft shoes were comfortable and in addition I had bought some tennis pumps. Although Trigger was not tired – he snorted, trotted and cantered – I dismounted for the sheer pleasure of walking in soft pumps with my jacket off without a care in the world. Trigger pressed on and I wished that he would always walk so fast.

Descending a steep, wooded ravine to the Tiber I heard a woman's voice calling to me. She was sitting on the roadside at the edge of the wood, a small attaché-case by her side. At first I thought she was waiting for a bus but I had not seen any buses on the road. She smiled and spoke to me. I went across the road to see what she wanted. She had jet black hair and a fine line ran from the corner of each eye. Her Italian face was so beautiful that I longed to sketch it but I feared that she might be offended, or think I was rude. I could not help but ask her why she was waiting there. She smiled and made a gesture, touched her skirt, and I saw that underneath the skirt she had nothing on. I had no compunction now in asking if I could make a sketch of her face. She laughed and shrugged her shoulders. While I was making a quick portrait a car drew up and her interest was transferred to the man who got out. I left them together and on turning a moment later I saw them disappear into the wood. I saw two more such women half a mile further along the road, sitting with their cases and a rug by their side chatting and smoking together on the grass as if out on a picnic. Nymphs of the woods, modern style. I cannot say that I was shocked. I was rather amused. For me, at any rate, they were beautiful, tempting, they did not spoil the classic landscape. I was rather disappointed that I did not see any more. Apparently they haunted only that particular ravine.

We crossed the Tiber over the Ponte Felice in a deep valley and trekked towards Terni, sleeping in orchards or at the edge of cornfields. The sun was hot during the day but the nights were chilly. Oats were scarce and sometimes Trigger had to eat barley. Peasants had few buildings and the conical haystacks built around poles had nearly all been sliced away. Donkeys, mules and oxen were used and men

Photo: Heinz Glassel

Trigger climbs the steps to drink at the Augustus Fountain in Augsburg, Bavaria.

Photo: Roland Heinzl

Trigger pays his horse compliment to a sculptor in a park in Stuttgart, Würtemberg, Germany.

"I've seen this before!" Trigger reaches the North Sea at Oster after the Mediterranean and the Adriatic.

Photo: Bousson-Lemmens

Trigger jibs at the gangway to the Bristol airplane which is to ferry us across the English Channel. He does not like the close-up look of the giant wings. He has no ambition to be a mechanized Pegasus.

Back to snow in Yorkshire after fifteen months ride.

Photo: The Yorkshire Post

and women worked in the fields with primitive hand-tools. Trigger would greet a mule with a load of hay on each side and a man on top with a neigh of fellow-feeling and the man would greet me with *'Bon viaggio!'* Passers-by would ask, *'Dove va?'* – where are you bound for? or *'Lontano?'* A monastery bell was tolling as we got to the top of a hill on a Sunday morning and entered Otricoli. A market was being held, mules, sheep, cattle were being bought and sold, entire pigs roasted on spits were being carved up hot in the street and I had a slice for breakfast – delicious! Peasants were arriving on foot from miles around, some crippled, bent almost double. On the road to Narni Trigger kept stopping and kicking his belly. For the first time he was bothered with horse-flies. I dismounted and helped him deal with them.

The main square of the walled town of Narni built on top of a precipice was crowded with inhabitants in their best clothes enjoying Sunday evening leisure, standing outside cafés or sitting in chairs. Trigger drank at the fountain, I sketched, and as the sun was setting we descended the steep road and slept on the bank of the Torrente Aia, the lights of Narni twinkling high above us. The days were now sunny, the farms mostly smallholdings; wheat was cultivated as precious stalks, husbanded by hand, all the golden ears the same height in what were little more than gardens. The ears looked as if they had been counted. Women cut grass and clover on the roadside with sickles and gathered it into sacks. Riding in the warm sun, my bare arms resting on the soft wool of my sheepskin rolled inside out and laced on top of the oats bag in front of the saddle, I thought of the traders and pilgrims in the past riding together and talking as in the *Canterbury Tales* with no other sound than the hooves of horses. Approaching Terni I saw a factory chimney, one of the first I had seen since leaving the Loire in France. But after passing through the town we were again in a region entirely agricultural, peasants shouting to their oxen, 'Hu Ho! Hu Ho!' That night we slept in a mountain pass where peasants had built lean-to shelters as barns among the rocks, a craggy gorge, no grass, no water for Trigger, and yet in one or two small patches the peasants were growing wheat in the cream-coloured stony earth. Then we came to the village of Molinaco with a brand-new church, quite a big one for such a small village. There I bought fresh eggs to suck, cheese and bread and wine. On the steep, curving road a man from Perugia was selling copper vessels and fire-irons, and in the fields shepherds stood leaning on their crooks watching flocks of sheep. In the old days the Via Flaminia went over the ridge but now a gallery has been tunnelled. Then comes a steep descent, the road curving full circle, and here we encountered a cloud-burst, rain and hail falling in a terrific downpour. We squeezed under a small yew, water pouring from the brim of my panama, and I could hardly see for rain. Then suddenly the sun came out in a blue sky with birds singing and a cuckoo calling.

Thunder and a menacing sky hurried us into Spoleto where I found shelter for Trigger under the archway entrance to a tree-shaded courtyard of an *albergo,* and here we stopped for several hours. After a meal in the *Trattoria Tre Fontane* I did some sketching in the rain, standing in a doorway in the Via Monterone.

It seemed that the rain was never going to stop so we rode on until darkness. Trigger found a small side road but a barking dog made us decide to turn back. The only place now was a small bit of level grass under some bushes on top of the wall over the Via Flaminia and here we slept in the rain. Continuing at dawn already at half past six we turned off the road into a village. We were both hungry and thirsty; I had chewed some stale cheese and had given Trigger my bread, but we got some oats where donkeys with panniers were outside a store. A woman brewed tea for me from one of my tea-bags and the baker's shop was open. Trigger drank at the fountain and I mended a burst leather pouch and a saddlebag in the square with fishing line nylon. We were now right in the middle of Italy. The village folk crowded around us talking about 'the Englishman'. We left with full bellies in the sunlight and I had drunk coffee and a *mistra,* but before the end of the day it began to rain again. I had stopped in a small shop selling spaghetti and ravioli, Trigger neighed to me and I rushed out to throw the water-

proof cover over my saddle. The heavy rain in a few minutes
caused flood water to come into the shop from the road.
'*Brutto tempo!*' exclaimed the people and I heard the now
familiar talk about the year being the worst in living memory.
'*Cattivo!*'

In the night on the roadside, carabiniere woke me up in
the grass where we were sleeping and demanded *documenti*.
Trigger had heard the approaching footsteps in the grass
and had got up. I threw off the waterproof sheet which was
over my head because of the pouring rain. Three men in
uniform with revolver holsters were looking down at me. I
recognised a military policeman with a small black moustache
who had not smiled at me when we passed in Spoleto. He
had not replied when I said, '*Buon giorno*,' but had eyed
me with suspicion and had watched me out of sight. However they had to be satisfied when I produced my passport
and documents, but it was a nuisance unpacking my saddlebag in the drenching rain.

Next morning the rain produced a picture, for while
sheltering I sketched Trevi, a town built up a steep hillside
a mile or so away from the Via Flaminia. The comment of
a young woman who saw the sketch was, '*Bello!*' But she
went on : 'Beautiful from a distance is Trevi but ugly when
you get to it.' However, the local sparkling white wine tasted
like champagne.

Although it was summer and in Italy, my fingers were
numb with the chill weather. In the afternoon we came to
an ideal spot, a strip of grass with clover and lucerne about
ten yards wide, sheltered by shrubbery, and here the sun
was warm. Trigger could graze and roll, I could dry my
blanket and cape, and on the roadside there was a well. This
was the kind of stop Trigger and I dream about. Trigger
purred almost like a cat. Then, after several hours basking
– the sun became quite hot – a lovely sunlit road to the
village of Valtopina. In the setting sun the local priest was
watching his flock play cards at tables outside a café, a man
showed me where I could buy oats for Trigger, and I enjoyed wine, bread and salami. Then, to crown a day of happy
contrast, still climbing, we found a triangular field by a river

where we could sleep. The two schoolboy sons of the owner of the field, Angelo and Valerio Ornelli, brought into the field for me six eggs, a parcel of sandwiches of raw smoked ham, a bottle of wine and a bottle of beer. They lay prone watching me perforate and suck two eggs – 'Oo! Oh!' – watched me set up my easel, admiring everything I did, ran for a glass, kept pouring out wine for me, watched me wash some clothes in the river, poured out more wine. Soon they were joined by more boys, kneeling and lying at my feet, whispering to each other. Then Angelo suggested that I should stay at least two or three days. A woman with a scythe and sack, coming down the bank of the river, unloaded all her beans from her apron into my lap. Before dark the entire hamlet had assembled in the field.

But during the night, disaster. A violent storm, another cloud-burst, the torrent overflowed its banks, flooding the field. The peasants came running out of their houses to help me, some of my things were floating away in the darkness. We got out of the field and were given shelter in a cart shed where there was a wine press. The flood had come so quickly that all my things were wet through. Fortunately in June the nights are short. Half dressed as I was when I walked with Trigger up the road I changed into shorts, although these too were wet, and when dawn came with the promise of a hot day I prepared to dry all my things in the sun. The field where I slept sloped up to a wood. As the sun rose I spread my blanket over a bush and wearing my swimming costume, dried my underclothing on my easel; my saddle, saddlebags, jodhpurs, jacket and sheepskin dried on the ground in the sun. Trigger waded and drank in the river and grazed happily, and after a warm, lazy day we slept another night in the field, this time high up the slope, but careful to avoid the places where surface water from the wood in the flood had left trails of gravel and stones.

When we rode away along the Via Flaminia – which was built over two hundred years before Christ, and along which Roman soldiers marched to the Adriatic and perhaps rested and were caught by storms on the same bank of that river –

a boy and a youth rode ahead of us on bicycles with the news
of our approach. At each farm they stood with the peasants,
then pedalled eagerly past us again. The faces of the girls
were tantalizingly beautiful, their eyes looking candidly
straight into mine as if reading my innermost thoughts, and
constant sleeping in the open has an aphrodisiac effect
on me.

The mineral springs in those hills are mildly radio-active
and therapeutical. In Nocera Umbra water is bottled. From
that mountain town we rode on towards Gualdo Tadino.
Assisi was not far behind us as the crow flies. The road zig-
zags and writhes through high wooded valleys. Some nights
we slept among brambles and Trigger got his long tail fast;
one night we slept on concrete slabs and I dreamt of snakes
and scorpions and woke up believing I heard a distinct hiss
but Trigger was peacefully snoring, legs outstretched.

At Gaifana I bought oats from a mill worked by a water
wheel. The skin of a badger was nailed to the veranda, and
women were washing clothes on a slab by the stream.
Farther along the road a woman who was returning from
the fields to her cottage walked by my side. Her curiosity
turned to commiseration when I answered that I had been
travelling nearly twelve months. She was anxious to make
coffee for me but I asked her to brew tea from one of my
bags. The door of her house was made of heavy horizontal
slabs of wood. It was the first time I had been in a small
Italian cottage. She opened what looked like cupboard doors
in a corner of the room, lit a fire of sticks on the stone floor
and placed an iron pot of water on a hook in the chimney.
When she had brewed my tea she put spaghetti in the pot
but I had left before this was ready. I was not hungry, and
Trigger was snorting with terror as two long-horned enormous oxen were passing slowly drawing a cart. That night
on the roadside where we slept fireflies were flitting everywhere; I have never seen so many. Their tiny lights sparkled
over Trigger who lay in a white heap by my side and when
I sat up one fell from my shoulder. We were wakened by the
loud braying of a donkey near by and the voices of peasants.
I had not seen a horse since we left Rome. I thought I saw

one coming along the road, trotting in the shafts of a cart but it had longer ears than a pure-bred horse.

We crossed a bridge over a deep ravine under a beetling cliff of rock, a torrent roaring below, then came hairpin bends descending into a wide valley. Far ahead was a much higher mountain range which according to my map must be the one where the Via Flaminia passes through the Gola del Furlo, Mount Pietralata on one side and Mount Puganuccio on the other. The cream sandstone dazzled my eyes with refraction from the bright light of the hot sun and lizards darted over the rocks. Tar was melting on the road. I noticed that one of Trigger's shoes moved slightly when he trod and we had still 70 kilometres to go to Fano. My new jodhpurs were fraying and I was low in cash.

From time to time Trigger suddenly stopped and kicked. Another of those horse flies on his belly. I swotted it. Another on his chest. Trigger got that with a biff of his nose, but he could not get at the flies on his belly with his tail or his nose because of the saddlebags. I felt sorry for Trigger, sweating under his saddle and tormented with flies. From time to time I refreshed his eyes with a moist sponge but he did not like me to sponge his nose. I was glad that I had dumped the breast collar along with other unnecessary weight. I had intended to sew lambskin on the breast collar but that would have made him sweat even more. According to the newspapers there was now a heatwave in Rome with temperature up to nearly a hundred degrees. Ahead of us was a chain of mountains, the last until we reached the Alps. The Italians always said, *'Piu avanti'* when I asked them how far it was to the next village where I could get Trigger a bucket of water. This is supposed to mean 'just a little further ahead' but it usually turned out to be about five miles. In Italy they do not tell the truth when talking about distance but instead of stretching it they dock it down. The only word that means what they say is *'Piano'*, – 'slowly'. *'Piano, piano!'* 'Slowly, slowly, take it easy.'

I was now wearing as little clothing as possible – just a

pair of shorts and a short-sleeve shirt. It was so hot it was difficult to believe that there had been a time when I wore a sheepskin jacket over thick woollen clothing, and a woollen cap instead of a panama hat.

In the little village of Pontericcioli I put Trigger in the shade and wolfed down a dish of spaghetti at the risk of being broke. The oats we bought at the *Consorzio Agrario,* in Scheggia were nearly done. Hurray! The owner bought a sketch I did of his café with him smiling at me behind his bar.

'No oats in this village, Trigger, but we'll get some more *piu avanti.*'

'Hurrrrrh!

A soft balmy breeze was blowing in the mountain pass, sensual to feel between the fingers. We found a disused quarry where grass was growing. I tethered Trigger to a honeysuckle bush for the night. The breeze was warm and everything that touched my skin gave me pleasure. During the night the south-west wind reached gale force but it was warm and pleasant. The long, lonely, treeless descent next morning reminded me of the end of the Georgian Military Road through the Caucasus towards Vladikavkas, and this too was a military road, it was an old Roman military road, and at the town of Cagli is a bridge dating back to A.D. 27. We made straight for an agricultural store to buy oats, but '*Chiuso . . . festa . . . Corpus Domini.*' Trigger's face fell. He understood 'Closed' – 'Holiday'. But we had luck A little farther along the road was a mill. All they had was flour of oats, some maize, and '*granoturco*'. This was better than nothing. Mixed with a little water it made a meal for Trigger. However now there was luscious grass on the roadside. After Acqualagna the mountains closed in on us. We had reached the gorge or 'throat' of Furlo.

It was frightening as darkness came. Just the road and a river, with sheer cliffs on each side, the jagged tops so high as to be almost out of sight. Where could we sleep? It was so forbidding I hesitated to go any further before daybreak, we were trapped in the narrow pass. I did not want to go back to Acqualagna but there was a *trattoria* at the mouth of the pass so I turned back to this restaurant which I noticed had a terrace. My idea was to sleep on the terrace when the restaurant closed. When I asked what time they closed, the reply was, 'Mezzanotte', midnight. Just after midnight, when all lights had gone out and Trigger's white robe was all that I could see in the dark pass, the craggy summits silhouetted against the stars, I led Trigger quietly on to the terrace. Before we lay down I gathered what I could of withered leaves and put them on the pavement for Trigger, and there we slept until dawn.

We had not gone far in the morning when the sun began to catch the tops of the highest rocks of the summits and these threw their weird shadows on those farthest west. What a dramatic scene! It might have been the entrance to a fabulous region. What must the Roman soldiers have thought on seeing this awe-inspiring pass for the first time? The immense rocks are pink, cream and grey, reaching up sheer, almost shutting out the sky in the narrow pass. It made me think of the imagined scenery of Dante's Vision. It was like the setting for some superhuman event. I stared ahead, turned and looked back, spellbound. Whether Trigger felt awe at this powerful appearance that we were not only seeing but experiencing I do not know. There was no vegetation, nothing moved except the shadows, our footsteps on the smooth level road at the bottom of this chasm rang lonely, the only sound. Even the dark green water below the smooth road was still. In silence the sun's rays crept down the pink cliffs turning them to orange, but like a curtain coming to close the vision a mist began to follow us, deep down in the fissure below the sun's rays, as if having failed to prevent our escape it was now trying to veil what we had seen with mortal eyes.

The deep level road passed through a gallery and we saw the sun.

CHAPTER NINETEEN

The Adriatic

We were now on the other side of the Apennines, the massive mountains towering behind us. Our next trial was that of heat. Trigger had shed all his winter hair, there was nothing else to shed. After the flood at Valtopina, I had tried travelling in shorts. My legs were sunburnt but now the sun was so hot I had to put on my jodhpurs. Some of the mules were wearing straw hats. I asked a peasant where I could buy one. He said he had made it. I rested Trigger in the shade during the hottest part of the day. The nights were cool. Stars in the southern constellations were higher than in England. The golden sunlight drenched the ripe wheat and the carpet of chequered fields – the cream-grey hay, the greenish yellow gold barley, the brownish old-gold heavy wheat. The mountains left behind were lilac. So powerful the colours, so exuberant the vegetation, no wonder the peasants were gay in plying me with wine, refilling my glass when I was not looking until I fell on the grass.

Arriving in Fano I rode under the arch of Augusto and hesitated at a crossing. I had now come to the end of the Via Flaminia. We had reached the Adriatic. Italians came to help me. 'Il palazzo Saladini? This way.' The Duchess of Montevecchio whom I had met in San Remo had invited me to her palace. It was not far away, in the Piazza Costanzi in the centre of the old town. The major-domo of the palace met me, took hold of Trigger's bridle and led us along a street to a stable where Trigger drank a bucket of water and thrust his nose into a manger full of fodder, and I was conducted to a restaurant. The duchess had been away and had not yet arrived but was expecting us. While I was dining, a fair man with a beard, wearing a broad-brimmed peasant's straw hat, introduced himself as Tom Storer, an Englishman who had married into the Montevecchio family. He had come to welcome me. He sat down with me and told me he was an artist. During our week's stay in Fano I enjoyed Tom's company, drinking tea with him in his studio or accompanied by his wife, Maria, having coffee under the strong scented limes in the square. A great fuss was made of Trigger, especially by the younger Montevecchios at the palace, Francesco and Maria Chiara. The dowager duchess, Matilde, whom I had met before, had been travelling to escape the freak weather, especially the cold. She told me that she had been to the Canary Islands, even San Remo made her shiver. As in Rome I slept with Trigger, but here in Fano we were able to bathe each morning in the sea. Before we left Fano, Tom made me a present of the painting I liked best, a picture he had done of the Roman pavement at the very end of the Via Flaminia– rather an appropriate one for both Trigger and me! It was packed and sent to England together with a crayon drawing which Maria Chiar did specially for me. In Fano, with the great approval of Trigger, I made a bonfire of papers, books, and winter clothing to reduce weight, and we rode away up the coast light-heated and light-loaded.

We spent twelve days riding up the coast to Venice, bathing in the sea each day after warm nights in the open, but as if the freak weather in Italy was determined not to let us escape without a finale never to be forgotten we were caught in the cyclone in the valley of the Po. Poor, terrified Trigger broke all his harness. I let him follow his instinct as trees were cracking and falling. He galloped into a cutting by the road among low bushes and there we crouched. Neither Trigger nor I suffered injury but the vortex of the whirlwind which passed over Ferrara killed eight people and wounded seventy. The colour of the sky was frightening, it was like the end of the world.

The desolation immediately following this *tromba d'aria* reminded me of the result of a bombardment in a war.

Houses wrecked, agricultural machines smashed, trees down, motor boats blasted out of the river, cars blown off the road into fields. Sirens were hooting, carabiniere and Red Cross vans arriving, men shouting, women weeping. Cold, heat, hardship, hunger, thirst, fatigue, danger shared had brought Trigger and myself close together; the tornado brought us even closer together by fear.

On the way up the coast from Fano, when we had got through the hills at Pesaro we often slept on sand. The country is flat with miles and miles of seaside holiday places, Rimini, Ravenna, and many smaller towns, the beaches crowded in the daytime but deserted at night. After the lido at Porto Garibaldi we slept on the roadside. Where the land was marshy, frogs were croaking in the reeds. Ditches again made it difficult. At one place to get to a dry spot I had to take everything off Trigger, risk him down a steep slope from a dyke and carry everything down myself. My sunburnt shoulders were sore. A pain in my face like neuralgia eased when I wore sun-glasses for a few days; I thought I had got sunstroke. On the bank of the immense expanse of water of the Lagoon between Chioggia and Venice, Trigger was tormented almost beyond endurance by horse flies and I was anxious when he became covered with lumps as big as marbles, but they disappeared after a few days. It was a long, lonely, weary two-day ride round the Lagoon. Mosquitoes bothered us in the night.

I could not take a horse into Venice, of course, so I rested him a few days at Mestre and went into Venice each day by bus and water-bus to paint. I wanted to build up my funds before riding to the Dolomites. We slept in the corner of a camping ground among motorists with blue and orange coloured tents from all over Europe, chiefly from Germany and Scandinavia.

I loved the painting and sketching in Venice and longed to stay, but Trigger could not be with me among the canals and we had a very long way to go before winter. The fierce sun, cold draughts of wind, and dazzling light were sometimes trying but the contrasts were stimulating, especially the violent contrasts of light and shade, the *chiaroscuro* of the

Italian scene, the exciting stereoscopic vistas. Unlike the intimacy of the spirit in the soft, veiled, hazy scenes of England, so subjective, so suggestive of what is hidden, Italy does not suggest to me anything hidden at all, it is objective, material, external. It is hard, bold, unveiled, naked, and almost strident in the north. In Rome, too, there is that sense of nakedness in a strong light, material bodies in the round, revelling in nakedness, classical; the mystery of half-veiled romance, of suggestion, blown away by the sirocco and all revealed, all said and done, nothing left to the imagination. But how beautiful the forms, the shapes, the colours so nakedly and violently thrust upon me! The impression comes with a shock. No wonder the classical sculptors, painters and poets responded to this brazen, glaring, open, shameless living panorama. It needs no ghosts to tell, the meaning is plain to see on the sunlit surface, the unreserved outspokenness of Italian nature.

Leaving Venice behind I rode across the plain of Lombardy towards the Dolomites. After passing Treviso the days were less hot. Trigger had stood up well to the extremes of climate and there was now a cool breeze and running water. Abundant clover and tall lucerne grew all along the roadside. Mount Grappa came into sight along the river Brenta on the third day. We were glad to leave the plains. The roofs of the houses were sloping slightly now, some with gables overhanging small balconies. Although we were still in Italy the region was quite different from anything we had passed through before. We were approaching what was once Austria. Tobacco was being cultivated. Bats flitted in the night. The scenery was magnificent, rocks on summits sticking up in sharp points like needles, the road shaded by chestnuts, the lower slopes of the mountains covered with vines and olives. In a ravine Trigger waded in the river Brenta and we slept on the bank where Trigger sighed with pleasure as he laid his head in the deep grass.

We came to the old fort of Tombion. Before World War I this was the frontier of Austria. The massive walls of the

old fort still block the narrow deep pass except for the opening where the road passes through, holes for cannons on
the Italian side, barracks and stables behind.

On the road to Trento my ear caught the dreaded click
of a loose shoe. It was the right anterior, shod in Fano, and
it was serious because the front nails were holding and beginning to break the front of the hoof. I had had my doubts
about the old farrier in Fano who kept missing the nails with
his hammer and the clinches were low down. Some spare
rubber cushions which I had bought in France may have
caused the shoe to come loose. Anxious to preserve Trigger's
hoof I stopped at once and considered whether to tether
Trigger, get a lift on a car and bring a farrier. We were miles
from the next town. Luckily a passer-by on a bicycle told me
of a village under a mountain not very far away where there
was a farrier. The shoe brought me luck, otherwise I would
never have seen this picturesque village with its steep streets.
The farrier removed Trigger's shoes, cut his feet back and
re-shod him and I got rid of the rubber cushions, all for only
600 lire. The whole village turned out to watch the shoeing
in the crowded yard, and what hospitality was lavished on
me! – wine, salami, ham, cheese, butter, cottage bread, and
Trigger was given hay and oats. We left the village, happy
but reluctant, at sunset, the church bell tolling, shadows
deepening among the mulberry trees and pines.

Sometimes when asked, 'Where are you going to sleep
tonight?' I have replied, 'That is a professional secret,'
because sometimes Trigger and I sleep where we are not
supposed to be. On the other hand, as in the village of Castel-
nuovo, we might sleep on the village green, Trigger lying
down first and making himself comfortable in full view and
to the delight of onlookers. In Trento, however, we slept
hidden by trees in public gardens only a few yards from a
lamp-lit avenue. In close country we were like foxes, moving
and sleeping by stealth. It was Sunday morning when we got
up in Trento from our bed of soft cedar twigs. In the main
square a crowd of hikers with rucksacks were waiting for
a café to open. It was only six o'clock in this Piazza
Vittorio Emanuele where the hikers stood in red stockings,

buckskin shorts, with eagle feathers in their felt hats and
the conversation was mostly in German. But for some days
I had heard inhabitants speaking German. At Levico I talked
to an old lady who remembered the days before World War I
when 'everybody here spoke German and this was Austria'.
At Pergine we had crossed the watershed between the two
rivers, the Brenta and the Adige, and there in the mountain
air 5,280 feet above sea level while sketching I could smell
chicken roasting. This appetising odour of cooking at such
an altitude was irresistible and in a luxury hotel I ate
a thumping meal. Down in Trento at the foot of Mount
Calisio I did a sketch of the beautiful Neptune fountain.

From Treviso, for seven days we had been travelling west;
now we turned north up the valley of the Adige towards the
high Dolomites. In my saddlebag was a litre of wine, biscuits,
bread and salami and in Trigger's bag six kilos of oats. We
were independent now until at Bolzano, two days' ride but
seven miles along the road, the smell of cooking again tempted
me and in a German-speaking restaurant I was handed a
menu of *Schweinbraten, Kalbsbraten, Wienerschnitzel* by a
typical German woman. At Salorno I came across the first
signs on the road in the beautiful old Gothic alphabet:
SCHWARZER ADLER, *Fremdenzimmer,* etc., but the
names and words were also in Italian: *Aquila nera. Alloggio.*
And the street names were now displayed in the two languages. A *Gasthof* where I drank beer had heavy oak chairs
and tables, panelled walls, and wide wooden window
bottoms. Yes, and even a drinking motto on an oak beam –
'*Wer niemals einen Rausch gehabt der ist kein braver
Mann.*'[1] Hear, hear! And how different the acoustics. No
longer the swish of plastic strip curtains and loud, harsh
voices pitched in a high key, instead deep soft guttural
sounds coming out of a carpeted silence. In the cloistered
square more felt hats with eagle feathers, and tweed capes.
Quite naturally some of the people I talked to called Trento
'Trient' and Bolzano 'Bozen' and I had to be careful.

In Bolzano I bought a mouth-organ – I had sold two
pictures for a thousand lire each. Trigger pricked his ears

[1] He who has never been drunk is not a jolly good fellow.

and rather liked the sound of it. As well as singing to him now when he was tired I played the mouth organ. And for the first time on my ride a journalist interviewed me in German; although we were still in Italy, his newspaper was published in the German language. It was not so much a sense of gradually leaving Italy as a feeling of entering Austria without having passed through any customs barrier.

CHAPTER TWENTY

Austria

We were now riding up a steep narrow gorge high in the mountains with the river Eisack making the pass ring with the noise of its swift water. This was the road to the Brenner Pass. It was crowded with traffic passing between Austria and Italy, most of the passengers being tourists in cars and coaches, and intermittently the railway came into view. Trigger and I travelled slowly, sleeping at night on dewy grass. I remember a lovely morning by the foaming river wondering however we had deserved such happiness, rolling in the grass bathed in dew but no matter, sporting with Trigger, playing my mouth organ and singing *Stenka Razin*; the torrent singing too, its turquoise water foaming white over the boulders, the giant humps bristling with pine like the shoulders of bears, great white clouds half-way behind mountain summits, it was like being in a dream.

Each day the climb tired us but we stopped from time to time to rest at an inn. Cellarers wearing dark blue aprons over their buckskin leather shorts waited at the door, receiving us with jokes and gaiety. Drinking wine, I read in one inn a notice in German: 'Credit given only to customers eighty years old accompanied by their parents.' But more often than not payment for my wine was refused and my glass refilled. But it was impossible to buy oats. Trigger had to live on grass and a little barley, but he got a good feast of hay and a rest when an Austrian-born baron invited us to his castle near Bressanone. His father, Baron Unterrichter, had been a cavalry officer of Austrian dragoons and 'had once ridden from Vienna to Berlin in seventy-two hours, where his horse dropped down dead'. This for me was a sad story; although the time was improbable the death of the horse was no doubt true. I don't like these record speed triumphs at the expense of a horse. Dick Turpin would have expiated his crimes and become a hero for me if he had given in before Black Bess died. Man has much to answer for in his treatment of horses.

Trigger and I took two days to ride from Bolzano to Brenner. But we got there before some of the passengers by rail, car or motor coach. A terrific thunderstorm brought down part of a hillside and blocked the road and railway for two days, making world news. Trigger mounted the debris of mud, sand and rocks on his four feet and continued. When we got to the Austrian frontier barrier, the Austrian customs veterinary officer said, 'I have been here fifteen years and you are the first horseman to come through the pass.'

But this fact did not stand us in good stead. On the contrary. Although we had never been held up by weather or natural disasters we were now held up by bureaucracy. For seven days we were held up at the Austrian frontier in the Brenner Pass in the rain five thousand feet above sea level. I had provided myself with a veterinary certificate of health for Trigger at Sterzing near the frontier but as when entering Italy this was rejected as useless. Now I must not only have an Austrian veterinary certificate, but before being allowed this I must have many other things too, much more difficult to obtain. I was informed that before being allowed into Austria the authorities must have written confirmation from Bavaria that I would be allowed to enter Germany after crossing Austria. And it was politely hinted that Germany, in turn, would first require written confirmation from Belgium that I would be allowed to enter that country from Germany. This was something new to me.

Imagine my predicament, a horse and no shelter, no oats, no hay, hardly any grass, in the rain, in the Alps, in a pass as high as Mount Snowdon, needing now to get into touch with governmental authorities in several European countries, having to contact ministries in one country after another, none willing to move until the other moved, and meanwhile Trigger and I unable to move a step forward. It was a sort of chain reaction so I decided that it would be better to

start at the other end. From Belgium I should have to get
into England again, so the first thing to do was to get into
touch with the Ministry of Agriculture in London and work
backwards. Correspondence by post would take weeks or
even months and I did not know even the addresses, and
the Austrian veterinary officer said that he was not empowered
to help.

I have travelled twice round the world and have been in
thirty-two countries without ever having need to ask for help
from the British consular service but here it seemed to be
my best bet. Tethering Trigger to the heavy lid of a manhole
in the sparse grass of a railway siding where we slept during
the six nights in the Brenner Pass, I took the train to Innsbruck and visited H.M. Vice-Consul. It was a woman. She at
once got in touch with the Austrian authorities, then by long-
distance telephone with the British Consulates in Munich
and in Brussels, and with the Foreign Office and the Ministry
of Agriculture in London. The wheels began to turn, consuls
got in touch with ministries in Germany and in Belgium,
documents were sent by post from London to Innsbruck,
letters from Bavaria and from Belgium to Innsbruck and
finally at the end of seven days the barrier pole at the
Austrian frontier was lifted for Trigger to pass through. I
had to pay for all the telephone calls but that was fair
enough. It cost me six pounds. Fortunately I had been able
to do some sketching while waiting in the Brenner Pass,
despite the rain, and these pictures I sold quite easily to
tourists at the frontier and in Innsbruck.

How happy Trigger was to be moving again, and downhill
too, into Innsbruck. I saw by reading a plaque at Brenner
that Goethe in the Pass had been held up *one* night but that
was by mere darkness. Quoting from his *Reisebilder* the
plaque said, '... *und nun erwarte ich, dass der Morgen diese
Felskluft erhelle, in der ich auf der Grenzscheide des Südens
und Nordens eingeklemmt bin.*'[1]

It was easier in those days to travel with horses!

[1] '... and now I waited for morning to light up this cleft in the
rocks where I was stuck at the boundary between the south and the
north.'

On the way down we rode past a queue of cars, coaches and motor lorries at least two miles long. An English voice hailed me from a car with 'G.B.' on it: 'We saw you on the telly last week in England.' Another thought-provoking change from the days of Goethe! – living pictures now travel faster than persons.

We stayed three days in Innsbruck, sleeping on the out-skirts and riding in each day. One night we slept in a garden and two nights on straw in a farm building outside the Ferrari Hof where Franz Haller, the owner, was warmly hospitable. In Innsbruck we were able to buy plenty of oats. Heavy rain began to fall one day and continued all day. In the main street another voice called to me in English. It was a woman. On the roll behind my saddle was a small Union Jack. Like my hat and cape it was drenched with rain.

'Oh dear!' she said, 'your flag is getting wet.'

'Madam,' I said, 'it is not the first time the Union Jack has been wet.'

Despite the rain I think Trigger liked Austria after Italy. The oats were much better and they were crushed. I dare say he missed the bathes in the Adriatic but he was glad to leave the horse flies behind, and those funny little things that ran quickly down his legs when he got up after sleeping by the lagoon. I once found a leech under his belly near his sheath, sucking his blood. And he was always so frightened when he had to cross a Bailey bridge. The rattle of the loose planks as the automobiles ran over them was terrifying. And that whirlwind . . .

I had lost nearly a stone in weight, but Trigger actually appeared to have gained. What few Italian lire I had brought through the Brenner Pass had now been changed into Austrian schillings and I was receiving Austrian money now for my sketches. The miracle of the 'loaves and fishes' made me wonder every day. The German word *'nichts'* was often the answer when I asked how much I owed for a meal or for oats. 'Nothing.' In Italy it had been *'niente'* and in France *'rien'*. In Sterzing, where Trigger and I had been invited to sleep in a garden, I awoke to find a veterinary certificate, a parcel of food and a bottle of wine by my side. They had been placed there during the night while I was sound asleep. That was in South Tyrol. Now in North Tyrol the same miracle accompanied us and in my mind I sometimes said grace for me and Trigger for more than I really deserved.

Our first night after leaving Innsbruck was at Zirl where we slept in the only vineyard in North Tyrol and I was invited to dinner in the Weinhof hotel. Dawn brought a dazzling view of the snow-capped Dolomites. Still riding uphill the air was pure and the scenery magnificent, peak after peak appearing on the horizon clean white, while on the roadside were drinking troughs each with a large carved wooden statue on a post over it; one of these was of a man with an umbrella and with bottles sticking out of his pockets. These painted wooden carvings were not religious. Like the large and beautiful wall paintings they were romantic or humorous, or illustrating folklore. Even the local post office has its share of folk art painted on its outer walls in bright colours. On my white horse I had no feeling of incongruity. We were riding through fairy-tale land. I don't think I would have been very surprised if I had met a giant or a dwarf.

How rich is Europe, not only in its scenery but in the variety of its imagination in culture and civilization. Our long slow ride through Europe had given me plenty of time to think, and to see, and to meet the people – and what a variety not only of people but of peoples! – and all essentially European. My thoughts had been stirred by monuments of its history and by manifestations of its modern civilization. After our very intimate acquaintance with the Via Aurelia and the Via Flaminia and the sight of Roman viaducts we saw the Europa Bridge, a road bridge over half a mile long and three times higher than the highest factory chimneys. And now within a matter of days – even on horseback – we were riding through what seemed like fairy-tale land, romantic with freshly painted folk art. Oh, how rich is

Europe! In its variety of imagination, art, civilization and personal freedom it is the richest continent in the world, if not in gold.

Our next night's sleep was at Seefeld in a small meadow. Although we had arrived in the forenoon after riding through forests with wild deer the little mountain town with its bright inns and restaurants in the sunlight was so lovely we stayed all day. Morning was pure and beautiful with heavy dew and the deep bronze music of cow-bells. Then came more forest rides, with more wild deer, and with abundant clear springs of water among the rocks, silent and lonely, lovely for horse and man.

Approaching the Austrian-German frontier the towering mountains began to close in on us. It was early morning when we reached the frontier post. The German veterinary officer was expecting us and we had not very long to wait before he arrived. I changed my Austrian schillings into German marks and we passed through.

In a few minutes we were in Mittenwald. I entered a *Gasthof.* We were in Germany. Two men in Tirolese costume on a platform built of pine logs were playing a piano accordion and a zither. Music was coming from other inns and cafés, there was music everywhere.

CHAPTER TWENTY-ONE

The Danube and the Rhine

Before leaving Innsbruck I had considered the possibility of riding through the Oberjock Pass to Immenstadt and Lake Constance and then to the Rhine falls at Schaffhausen. There was still a possibility of joining that route via Füssen but Trigger had had enough of mountains and I had made up my mind to ride north. I had read in the newspapers of the disastrous floods in Germany caused by the freak weather and how crops had been ruined. There was no telling what else might happen so my intention now was to ride across the south German plain to Ulm on the Danube, and get nearer to the North Sea before winter. We could go via Kempten but I chose the slightly longer but easier route, and from Garmisch-Partenkirchen took the road to Munich. Again, by turning off at Oberau I could ride through Oberammergau to Augsburg without touching Munich but Trigger was due for shoeing again, Munich was nearer and it would be interesting to visit that great city of art.

If I had not chosen that road to Munich I might never have met Frau Wiest. How much chance is there in meeting? Or is it chance? The Greeks used to say, 'All strangers come from Zeus.' Surely it seemed to me that the hospitality of Frau Wiest for Trigger and me was another godsend. And our meeting happened in a very peculiar way. Trigger and I were both very tired. We had passed a very uncomfortable night trapped in the darkness with a wall, railway, river and marsh on one side of the road and a cliff of rock on the other, indeed we were lucky to get off the road at all. A muddy path led into a concave part of the cliff which was overgrown with jungle-like vegetation, stunted trees festooned with tough creepers searching for the sun and

which I had to cut away with my knife to enable Trigger
to lie down. Neither of us had slept a wink. Both of us were
so used to fresh air and an open sky, the fetid atmosphere
under those creepers was disgusting; but it was our only
place of safety from the heavy motor lorries on the narrow
road until daylight. Riding in the morning towards Munich
Trigger suddenly stopped. We had been riding for some
miles along a country road which ran alongside the modern
motorway. 'What's the matter, Trigger?' He was looking at
a small archway, apparently the entrance to a subway under
the other road. It was odd that he should be interested in
leaving the pleasant traffic-free and grass-bordered road that
we had now found. Out of curiosity I dropped the reins and
he at once entered the subway. At the other end he turned
the opposite way to Munich and after passing some workmen's
huts stopped at the door of a forester's house. It was a large,
substantially built house of stone like a small hotel bearing
the sign, 'Forsthaus. Rose Wiest'. A card in the window bore
the notice, in German, 'Day of rest'.

'It's shut,' I said to Trigger but he waited. And Frau Wiest
came to the door. 'My horse has brought me here, I don't
know why,' I laughed. 'I know,' said Frau Wiest. She led us
to a small fenced pasture with a well at the edge of the forest
and when I had unsaddled Trigger she said to me, 'Come in.'

It was more than a day of rest for us, we stayed three.
Frau Wiest is one of those rare women so deeply absorbed
in self-learned philosophy that I can best describe her as a
mystic. She not only gave me food, personally she gave me
comfort of the spirit. I found that she was a fellow traveller
– I don't mean 'fellow traveller' in the barbarous contem-
porary sense now used by politicians, I mean it as used in a
much deeper sense when words were still on the gold
standard, unadulterated. As I wrote in her 'Golden Book', she
is a fellow traveller 'on that wonderful path which leads
neither left nor right, nor north, south, east, or west, but
upwards at the crossroad'.

I slept with Trigger in the pasture. One morning when
I was getting up a man passed on horseback. I asked him
if he could tell me where I could find a farrier. He gave me

the address of one a few miles away and told me of a short
cut through the forest. 'Tell him to charge the shoeing to
my account,' he said and handed me his card – Doktor Thilo
Krieger. Frau Wiest described to me the way through the
dense forest and how I would know I was on the right path
if I passed a *Wald Kreuz* where foresters go to pray as there
is no church near. Trigger loved the ride through the forest
although from time to time his nostrils expanded and his
ears pricked. I had seen a notice at the entrance to the forest
warning people that there are wild boars and that they go
through the forest at their own risk. I dismounted at the
Wald Kreuz. It was a forest-cross of wood fastened to a tree,
a wooden ledge beneath it and a sloping wooden kneeler,
and it was fenced in with wooden rails and a rough wooden
gate. I entered, knelt and in the silence of the forest said a
little prayer for Trigger. It was the only church I entered in
my ride through Europe.

The farrier, Andreas Baur, was a young man with two
sons learning the trade – something rare in farriers today
anywhere. With new shoes and well rested, Trigger bore me
along the road to Munich. There were tears at the parting
with Frau Wiest and she embraced me tightly as she
whispered, '*Verwandte Seelen finden sich.*'[1]

In Munich everybody was telling me to visit the *Verkehrs-
ausstellung* – the International Transport Exhibition – which
was being held that week. Every kind of road transport; rail,
air, and sea, and even space-ships were on show. England
had sent a hovercraft. When we got there, Trigger, as 'transport' was the only living exhibit – an unofficial one. We were
photographed by the side of the American space rocket.
'This also is transport,' I said, patting Trigger. 'And not a
museum piece. Still in use and still going strong. But in one
hour and a half we travel seven miles while the rocket satellite
in the same time goes round the world.'

During the five days we spent in Munich I sketched and
sold some of my pictures and that was one of my reasons

[1] Sympathetic souls find each other.

for staying in a city. Finance was a constant need, especially now that with the exception of my sheepskin jacket I had dumped and burnt my winter clothes to save weight, and the clothes I had were wearing out. I could sell more pictures in a few days in a city than in weeks riding along lonely roads. At night I slept with Trigger on grass on the site where Hitler's Braunhaus used to stand. It is near the Königsplatz where there are trees, and public paths. The only time I was disturbed was when police drove up in a car and demanded, *'Was bedeutet dies?'*[1] When they found out who I was they smiled and wished me a good journey. The German who had recommended this place when he saw me looking for a patch of grass came back to me with a jug of hot coffee, sandwiches, a bottle of wine and a box of cigars, while another passer-by walked several hundred yards with a bucket of water from a restaurant for Trigger. Although the difference in language, food, dress, architecture and climate, was great, the spirit of hospitality was the same as in France and Italy. It any difference there could be it was in the material *quantity* of the gifts lavished on us – like the German love of the massive in everything! When we were leaving in the evening of the fifth day I was reminded that it was Friday the 13th. Although I am not superstitious there was Trigger to be considered. I pulled the rein and turned back. In any case we could not have got far before dark.

In Augsburg we halted for another three days, where again German hospitality exceeded anything we had experienced in other countries. The city's *Gartenbauamt* – its horticultural or parks office – because I slept with my horse in the open, invited me to sleep in their meadowland near the Tierheim, and there I was brought presents of food both for me and my horse. One man brought me a new headstall and halter for Trigger because mine was so very much the worse for wear. The crowning gesture of Augsburg's love came on the morning of our departure. A woman who had visited us each morning with her grown-up daughter bringing hot coffee from her home some distance away for fear that I should be feeling cold, threw her arms round me as if I

[1] What's the meaning of this?

were a child. And after I had saddled Trigger and was bidding good-bye, she once more took me in her arms and tearfully sobbed, 'Again I have him in my arms.' Such tenderness, although embarrassing to me as an Englishman, was very touching. Another meeting and parting that I shall never forget was in a small town on the way to Ulm. This time it was Trigger who was the object of such effusion of affection. A bare-headed young man in a tweed jacket and slacks stood by Trigger all the time we were stopped in the square, fondling his nose and whispering to him. Several times he dashed to a shop and bought packets of biscuits and fed them to Trigger. All this was done quietly and intimately while I was a long time writing a letter in a café. When I had posted the letter and was walking away with Trigger, the young man gave Trigger a final gentle pat and stood watching us go. I turned round several times and saw him standing there just in front of a little group in his sand-coloured tweed jacket, getting smaller and smaller, as we got farther away. He must have spent nearly all his money on Trigger and had had his arms round Trigger's neck; now he was dwindling into a speck of loneliness and we were getting smaller and smaller as Trigger disappeared from his sight and touch for ever.

When we got to Ulm it began to rain again and we had cloudy skies and rain almost all the way from the Danube to the Rhine. During our stay in Munich I had been able to have my monsoon cape cleaned and reimpregnated. The weather was warm, I was sunburnt and fit, under my waterproof cape much of the time on the road I was wearing nothing more than a cotton shirt and shorts, the passing lorries splashed me as they swished by like hovercraft, my wet cape flapped against my bare legs and my monocle dangled against my bare chest, but I did not care. There comes a time in constant rain when it no longer matters. I was drinking sunshine in the wine and walking by the side of Trigger, singing the popular song as my shoes splashed:

'Hüa-ho alter Schimmel hüa-ho ...'

The Schwabian dialect was still being spoken although we were now in Württemberg – 'Liaba trunka u, ghunka, als

noet trunka u, dennoch ghunka![1] I was very happy and
so was Trigger. The spire of Ulm cathedral, the highest in
the world, receded behind us and we splashed on towards
the Black Forest.

Trigger often seemed amused by my monocle but I had
to watch for him biting it. He did not understand that I
could not see the road signs without it. Trigger's eyes did
not need any help. Nor did mine when I was thirteen. I was
sixty-seven and my next birthday was only a few days off –
sixty-eight. I planned to give Trigger another bottle of champagne in his oats. He will not drink champagne but he will
eat it in his oats. But he will drink tea, coffee, milk, or
coca-cola.

Trigger liked Germany. The soil was much softer than
in Italy and Austria. And there were more horses. He met
and got to know quite a few. At an old brewery in Garmisch
where I was able to get some oats he spent a few happy hours
with five horses – Hans, Fritz, Max, Prinz, and Arak, while
I was drinking beer.

At Zusmarshausen a man named Dominikus Hander
opened a gate as we entered the little town and said: 'Come
in here'. He told us that Napoleon had stayed one night at
Zusmarshausen. Well we stayed two nights and Napoleon
could not have enjoyed greater hospitality. We were in a
fenced field with luscious grass and I had a hut with a deck
chair and a table covered with a cloth. Dominikus and his
wife and their neighbours brought soup, cooked meat and
vegetables, cake, wine, beer, cider, coffee, liqueurs and cigars.
I sat in the open air and had to shut Trigger in another field
until the table had been cleared. I pulled his leg by telling
him that he had gout and he must not have wine despite
the Schwabian 'Gout sufferer's motto'. When I bent down

---

[1] 'Better to drink and limp than not to drink and still to limp.'

and felt at his tendons, playfully, as if looking for a fault I thought of the poem I had seen in Munich:

Wer Pferde ohne Fehler sucht
Und Mädchen ohne Mängel
Hat nie ein gutes Pferd im Stall
Und im Bett 'nen Engel.

He who seeks a fautless horse, and a girl without a blemish, has neither a good horse in t'shed, nor in bed an angel.

Riding north through Württemberg from Hohenzollern through Baden and then Hessen we crossed the Rhine into Pfalz, via Esslingen, Stuttgart, Heilbronn and Heidelberg, meeting with wonderful hospitality all the way. Along the valley of the Neckar we slept on the bank each night, the slow barges chuffing by. Sometimes there was rain but always the valley was lovely and the leisurely speed of the barges was more in keeping with our own old world speed. Apart from the occasional mad rush of a car, with tyres screeching round bends, all was in harmony. Gifts from the people were so abundant we had no room to carry them all. Near Stuttgart in a village inn an ex-cavalry man insisted that Trigger could carry more and when I went outside I found that he had strapped another leather pouch to the saddle. It was a German cavalry pouch and when I opened it I found cigars, a bottle of Schnapps, cigarettes, some sausage sandwiches with rye bread and a sour gherkin. 'Every day is like Christmas!' I exclaimed. The donor came out, patted Trigger, saying, *'Sieht gut aus. Gut genährt.'*[1] Riding by a factory in the rain a shout came from the office and I was given coffee and whisky while the manager went in his car to get a sack of oats for Trigger. With the sack over the saddle I walked the few miles into Stuttgart where we stayed two days.

[1] He looks well. Well nourished.

Approaching Heidelberg we stopped at a lay-by where a bench and a rough table stood on the bank of the Neckar and here, while we were having lunch, a young couple in a car wanted us to stay the night at their house where they had land. When I excused myself the man drove off and returned with a bottle of wine, tinned food, bread, a pair of shoes and a shirt which he insisted on giving to me. The problem was where to put all these things. When Trigger had eaten his oats I hung his empty nosebag on my folded easel which stuck out of my saddlebag and carried these extra presents in there until I had drunk the wine and eaten the food. Trigger helped me to deal with the bread.

We stayed a night and a day at Worms where in the sixteenth century Martin Luther made his famous confession of faith. We were guests of a man who met us in his car on the road and invited me to bring Trigger to his riding stables. In the evening I was invited to a party in his house where we drank Pfalz wine. His wife, mother-in-law, and daughter were there, and during the conversation I was astonished when one of the guests left us for a while and my host remarked casually, 'He is a very rich man. He has a brothel here with twenty-five women.' His mother-in-law nodded and repeated, 'Yes. Twenty-five women.' These remarks were made as calmly and casually as if saying, 'He has a garage here and twenty-five taxicabs,' or, 'a chain of twenty-five grocer's shops'. They were quite respectable citizens who were talking and they went on casually to talk of something else.

Northwards to Mainz the country was flat and monotonous and almost entirely covered with vineyards, although smoke was rising from the burning of rotten straw from the crops ruined by the disastrous floods of the summer, and there was an acute scarcity of oats. Some of the fields were still under water. Trigger was frightened by the firing of guns on ranges by American tanks. There was no scarcity of wine however and I was guest one night at a *Weingut* where the owner took me into the enormous cellar under the wine-press to taste the various brands. In a rack were 3,000 bottles. I was told that altogether some 80,000 bottles were in store.

Trigger meanwhile was enjoying the company of a mare called Lotte. Great excitement was caused when a black maria drove through the street, the police announcing through a loudspeaker that the local bank had been robbed and asking for help in arresting the robbers.

It was a relief to see rising ground again between Mainz and Bingen, and quite a shock when riding into a square full of schoolchildren to see a chestnut tree all brown. All of a sudden it was autumn. A woman came to me and entreated me to come under a bedroom window where a sick child could look out and see Trigger. A pale face appeared at the window and smiled. I sent a sketch of Trigger up to him and played my mouth organ for him under the window.

At Mainz the Rhine widened with the influx of the Main and from then on we rode close to the river's left bank; after Bingen for many days we rode almost at the water's edge, the Rhine barges passing swiftly downstream or toiling slowly upstream, flying flags of Switzerland, Holland, and other countries, music coming from the white and gold passenger boats. Each night we slept on the bank, finding some place where at a bend in the river there was room between the road and the Rhine.

At Märchenhain, a little place under the vine-terraced slope below a castle, Trigger and I brought real romance to a model fairy-tale land. In little caves and on ledges of the rocks and terraces were painted wooden or plaster figures of Snow White and the Seven Dwarfs, the Pied Piper, Sleeping Beauty, and others so beloved by children. Sitting on a bench overlooking the Rhine I thought of our ride through Europe which had already taken more than a year. What ingredients for a fairy tale! A white horse from England with a Cinderella past heralded by a horn, a princess with a dragon on her crest, a castle with an open window, a diamond studded horse shoe, a moving mountain, a whirl-wind, sirens in a ravine, a Black Forest . . . a true tale, and what was ahead of us I did not know.

And here we were, about to ride past the rock of the Lorelei in the gorge of the Rhine with a castle on one bank called 'The Mouse', and one on the opposite bank called

'The Cat'. Then there was the Mouse Tower with its legend of wickedness. Horses must have had a tough time before the barges were powered by engines. A large painting on an external wall of the Landsknecht Hotel shows three power-ful horses pulling a barge upstream. There is no tow-path now. At Trechtingshausen Trigger had a narrow escape from being killed. We had slept on the river bank and I was letting him graze when he suddenly took it into his head to walk up the path to the railway crossing. I ran after him in my bare feet and caught him just in time; there are no gates, and trains pass every few minutes – the rail traffic on both banks is almost continuous night and day.

The town of Oberwesel was decorated with flags and gay with music, the streets crowded with happy people celebrating their Weinfest. The hill, terraced with vineyards, leaves only just room at the foot for one long main street and some short ones sloping down to the water. Along the main street on each side were shelters built of wooden battens, vine branches and canvas, and inside were joyful men and women, sitting on benches and drinking wine from the tops of huge barrels which served as tables, local townsfolk and honoured guests from the neighbouring towns of Kaub, Bacharach, Boppard and St Goar. The rain was pouring down but it did not damp the high spirits of the Rhine-landers.

And so we followed the sinuous wide river which gleams snake-like between the beetling cliffs, the moon rising at night over the castled summits of the Taunus mountains, the coloured navigation lights of the barges serpentining in the dark waters, the threshing of the propellers of the Rhine steamers passing close to us. Then in the early morning awakening with the Rhine all to ourselves I watched the dawn from my blanket.

Coblenz, Bad Godesberg, Bonn, Cologne; then began our ride west to the Belgian frontier.

CHAPTER TWENTY-TWO

Waterloo

It was with a thrill that I first saw on the horizon ahead the foothills of the Ardennes. Although I was sorry to leave Germany, and I had felt the same on leaving France and Italy and Austria, I knew that we were getting nearer England again. Welling up into my anticipation now was a feeling of triumph. But when I looked at the kilometre stone, multiplied it by five and divided by eight, that twinge of sadness came. Only twenty miles of Germany left. I began to listen more closely to the Platt Deutsch, sip slowly the German beer. I was leaving this hospitable land, maybe for ever.

But it was not until we got to Verviers that I began to hear only French spoken around me. The first signs of Belgium began at Limburg with the two or three storey brick houses with white facings round doors and windows. It had been unexpectedly easy to cross the frontier. The veterinary certificate given to me in Aachen by a German vet who charged no fee was recognized and accepted by the Belgian customs without fuss. I had not slept in a bed since that camp bed in Genoa and after a night in a field just over the frontier I again slept in the open in the paddock of a riding school near Limburg on the Route de Bellevaux. This was the first riding club I had come across since leaving the Ligurian coast, seven months before. An escort of honour rode with us from the club into Verviers and I was given quite a banquet. And near Verviers Trigger was shod again. Then we rode on to Liége.

Instead of riding direct to Brussels from Liége we made a detour and visited the field of Waterloo, and I slept with Trigger two nights on the battlefield. In many ways this was

the culmination of my European ride. Waterloo has sometimes been called 'the crossroad of Europe'. The thoughts
that came to me while spending these two days with
my horse on the battlefield will not be forgotten. It was
as if Trigger shared my pilgrimage. Probably we are the first
man and horse to sleep together in the grass under the stars
since Waterloo. The first to rest in that hallowed spot alive.
Never have I felt so close to another world since that unofficial armistice that I arranged between the trenches at Festubert nearly fifty years ago. It was Trigger by my side that
stirred this inner awareness of another, a greater world.
Trigger, and a Belgian whom I met, Norbert Brassinne,
a Belgian with French partisan feelings, a worshipper of
Napoleon. Norbert was born in a house by the sunken road
where his ancestors had lived for generations. He knows by
tradition every inch of the battlefield. In the fading light
at dusk he led me and Trigger across the stubble to a large
hollow in a field. 'It is not generally known,' he whispered,
'that four thousand horses are buried here.' We were silent
for a while. Trigger by my side was perfectly still in the
fading light. He might have sensed our gravity, his head was
down a little. 'Where is the monument?' I asked. Norbert
shrugged his shoulders. 'There isn't one.'

Under the sod were English horses, French, German . . .
lying together. At peace now. Horses are not political but
they are more loyal than men. I remembered the many pictures I had seen of poor, brave, wounded horses piling up
on top of each other in the sunken road. How merciful is
death. How peaceful is the grave. The battlefield is dotted
with monuments to *men*, but . . .

During the night as I lay awake I could see the pyramid
with the Lion silhouetted against the stars and I was lying
in the grass near where Wellington stood. Trigger was a
white heap lying by my side. But I remembered how he stood
riderless in the dusk by that hollow. And I thought of all the
other horses all through history who have been faithful to
man. How appropriate it would be to have a monument
erected to them at last. And how fitting it would be to erect
it on the field of Waterloo where so many horses gave their

lives. A monument not only to the horses that fell there but to all horses in history who have fallen in battle in their loyalty to man. I am not a rich man but there are many horse-lovers in the world. As I lay there I imagined a great gathering of horsemen from many countries. I saw them dismount and walk slowly past an unveiled monument to the music of a funeral march. After contemplating the idea I even heard music in my imagination: Trombones—

A monument to *all* the brave horses of history who have fallen in battle...

If I can bring it about... how appropriate that it should be inspired by Trigger, an ex-rag-and-bone horse.

We had approached the field of Waterloo from Rixensart, riding across the fields the way that Blücher came. I bought oats at an old corn mill still worked by a water-wheel, the miller boasting that his mill had ground oats for Blücher, but the farm of Hougoumont today is cultivated by machinery and although the bullet holes are still there and apertures in a brick wall for cannon I could hear the sound of an electric milking machine. Carved on a slab of stone are the words of Napoleon: *'La terre paraissait orgueilleuse de porter tant de braves.'*[1] He knew how to talk to soldiers.

Leaving the field at Braine-l'Alleud we rode north towards Brussels stopping on the way in the town of Waterloo to visit the old *Quartier Général* of the Duke of Wellington, then

[1] 'The earth appeared proud to carry so many brave.'

northwards through the forest, sleeping a night just south of the capital, and entering Brussels in the morning. There two cars met us from Hilversum to do a film for Dutch television and to be shown in other European countries with captions in various languages. Trigger had become a European television star. In my interview I promised to do what I could to remove the blinkers from Britain as I had done for Trigger. We had brought something with us from Britain and were taking something of continental Europe back with us. The interview took place in a street in the middle of Brussels and when I said this the crowd applauded. Of course Britain is an integral part of Europe and we British are much more European than many of us realise.

North of Brussels we entered the Flemish-speaking part of Belgium, almost another country. The sudden almost complete change in language is striking. Newspapers too were now printed in Flemish and Trigger's name became *'Trekker,'* and as a horse having been called a *'cheval'*, a *'cavallo'*, a *'Pferd'*, a *'Schimmel'* and a *'Gaul'* he was now a *'paard'*.

Farmers all over Belgium had suffered from the disastrous weather of 1965 and were calling for further help from the government. The Belgian army helped in trying to save the harvest after appeals from as many as three hundred communes, and soldiers had given nearly fourteen thousand man-hours of work. We spent seven days riding along country roads from Brussels to the coast, through Alost, Ghent, Ecklo, Maldegem and Bruges. Apart from fog the weather was fine and we had no difficulty in finding fodder. The hospitality of the people was warm and generous. At Ostend the owner of the hotel *H.M.S. Vindictive* actually rolled out a red carpet for us! He invited Trigger in too, and to the delight of everybody Trigger walked up the carpet and had breakfast with me in the hotel. In addition to his oats and a bowl of water he had apples and carrots and he stole my bread.

We stayed in Ostend a week as Trigger had to submit to a mallein test and await the result of the injection of the serum in accordance with the regulations for entering into England. Fortunately the test proved negative, otherwise it would have meant quarantine. We stayed at the riding school called

Manège des Drags in the Avenue de la Reine, an enormous group of buildings which were formerly royal stables presented to King Leopold by the King of Norway. I slept with Trigger in the open in the paddock. Every day we bathed in the sea together.

The crowning gesture of hospitality came when at the end of our long ride through continental countries we were honoured by being given a free passage by air to England. A special transport plane came from Lydd for us and the burgemeester, the mayor of Ostend, came to the airport to see us off. He shook hands with me on the tarmac and embraced Trigger, but Trigger eyed the giant Bristol plane with suspicion. He had never been so close to a plane before and his worst fears were aroused when it became clear to him that he was expected to go aboard. He shied at the narrow gangway. Against my advice the strongest porter took hold of Trigger's halter and tried to pull him towards the gangway but in a tug of war between a horse and a man the horse is bound to win. Finally I got him aboard by mounting, riding him round the plane several times under the enormous spread of wings and then suddenly up the gangway. He was accommodated in a large steel box bolted to the floor. The pilots climbed the companion-ladder to the upper deck and entered their cabin. An air hostess came to the steel box and fondled poor Trigger, but although he had had many strange adventures this aircraft was something quite new, and he jerked his head away from her and looked through the windows with apprehension. When the engines started up he trembled, his eyes dilated. The powerful engines revved up. What a din! He could see through the windows as the plane began to taxi along the runway, the noise of the engines increasing, until they were deafening, the vibration shaking the whole plane. I tried to talk to him, play my mouth organ, but he could not hear me. Then with a thundering shuddering roar we took off. We were airborne. The vibration ceased and Trigger quietened down, but when I gave him a sugar-lump it fell out of his mouth.

The plane flew along the coast over the land almost as far as Calais before its course brought us over the sea. Trigger appeared agreeably interested. We could see through the low windows the toy-like houses and the thin white roads that called for no effort now. The cattle in the fields were mere dots. We were almost back over the point where we had started our continental journey fifteen months before. He had no time to be worried about the sea for in a few minutes we could see England below us. I was surprised myself when the air hostess held up five fingers and we began to lose height. 'Five minutes,' she said. The plane banked gently, the green land rose up to meet us, and presently we touched down at Lydd airport.

Whether Trigger realised that he was on English soil again or not, he knew he was free from his box, and I had no difficulty in getting him down the gangway. When I mounted he reared and bucked with joy and crossed the runway at a gallop. Riding from the airport to Lydd I had to use the rein to keep him on the left side of the road and at junctions I sometimes forgot myself despite the signs in several languages – '*Tenez la gauche*', '*Links fahren*', 'Keep to the left'.

At the Rising Sun inn after giving Trigger his nosebag I enjoyed roast beef sandwiches, pickled onions and English beer. I decided to stay overnight at Lydd, the days being short now. The innkeeper's wife offered me a bedroom and was surprised when I told her that on my ride I had spent over four hundred nights sleeping in the open and that I intended to sleep out again with my horse.

We slept in the churchyard at Lydd in deep grass between the graves but before retiring something very unfortunate happened. While I was in the Rising Sun a thief outside in the darkness explored Trigger's harness and I was robbed of my waterproof cape, my camera and a purse with foreign money which were in a leather pouch. In the camera was a film with some photographs which I shall never be able to replace. The landlady of the inn was most indignant, the police were called, and she declared to me: 'If you open your mouth in Lydd they'll steal your teeth.' This picturesque exaggeration was unfair to Lydd, of course. As far as I am concerned there may be only one thief in Lydd and everybody I met there was kind, hospitable and friendly, but I felt sorry that this should have happened on the first night back in my native country.

The village of Lydd is not likely to forget that night. The arrival of a white horse from the continent by air, a police sergeant and a constable at the Rising Sun and a hurried search through the village for a thief. Next morning when I was getting up from my blanket among the gravestones an old man appeared on the path in the churchyard with his dog flabbergasted. 'What's this?' he gasped. 'A horse in a churchyard? I've nivver seen aught like it in all mi' eighty years!'

Riding across the Romney Marsh towards Ashford I soon got used to keeping to the left of the road instead of to the right. It took longer to get used to miles after kilometres, almost automatically I worked out that I was quite near to a place then suddenly remembered. Oh hell! they're *miles* not kilometres – which makes a difference on horseback. But what lovely names! Rye, Ivychurch, Appledore. And how lovely the countryside, the orchards, the hopfields again, and the turf, the soft turf, and English grass. The speed of cars on the country roads was more leisurely than in the continental countries. It was grand to be in England again.

But the nights were drawing in. It was November when we reached Yorkshire. After rain and fog, one evening in the darkness on a hill I felt a fresh touch on my hands and face. In the light of a road lamp I could see that it was snow. The soft feathery flakes fell silently. Trigger's ears twitched. He knew that it was snow. He had already grown his winter coat again. His mane was thick, his hair long over his girth straps and beginning to curl again on the muscles of his legs. The snowflakes were wandering. In the hush the sound of his footsteps grew quieter. Dancing, spinning, whirling came the crystals at differing angles and not falling straight in the still air, straying by such mysterious paths and yet the placing was just, the covering even. It was different from anything else as if coming from another region. This coming of the first snow was dignified, inevitable like fate, like death; regal, coming into its own like truth that bides its time and enters unhurried. The winds may blow it about but still it covers the earth, indifferent to the world.

I awoke in the middle of the night breathing the frosty air with gladness, Trigger snoring by my side. Then I remembered my difficult personal problem of making certain worldly ends meet and almost unconsciously murmured, 'O God give me grace!'

When I opened my eyes I could hardly believe what I saw. In a clear sky the full moon was silvering the snow-covered hills and icy rocks, and the bare trees were lace-like. Grace? That was grace. Grace abounding.

Other titles in the Equestrian Travel Classic series published by The Long Riders' Guild Press. We are constantly adding to our collection, so for an up-to-date list please visit our website: **www.thelongridersguild.com**

Title	Author
Southern Cross to Pole Star – Tschiffely's Ride	Aime Tschiffley
Tale of Two Horses	Aime Tschiffley
Bridle Paths	Aime Tschiffely
This Way Southward	Aime Tschiffely
Bohemia Junction	Aime Tschiffely
Through Persia on a Sidesaddle	Ella C. Sykes
Through Russia on a Mustang	Thomas Stevens
Across Patagonia	Lady Florence Dixie
A Ride to Khiva	Frederick Burnaby
Ocean to Ocean on Horseback	Williard Glazier
Rural Rides – Volume One	William Cobbett
Rural Rides – Volume Two	William Cobbett
Adventures in Mexico	George F. Ruxton
Travels with A Donkey in the Cevennes	Robert Louis Stevenson
Winter Sketches from the Saddle	John Codman
Following the Frontier	Roger Pocock
On Horseback in Virginia	Charles Dudley Warner
California Coast Trails	J. Smeaton Chase
My Kingdom for a Horse	Margaret Leigh
The Journeys of Celia Fiennes	Celia Fiennes
On Horseback through Asia Minor	Fred Burnaby
The Abode of Snow	Andrew Wilson
A Lady's Life in the Rocky Mountains	Isabella Bird
Travels in Afghanistan	Ernest F. Fox
Through Mexico on Horseback	Joseph Carl Goodwin
Caucasian Journey	Negley Farson
Turkestan Solo	Ella K. Maillart
Through the Highlands of Shropshire	Magdalene M. Weale
Wartime Ride	J. W. Day
Across the Roof of the World	Wilfred Skrede
Woman on a Horse	Ana Beker
Saddles East	John W. Beard
Last of the Saddle Tramps	Messanie Wilkins
Ride a White Horse	William Holt
Manual of Pack Transportation	H. W. Daly
Horses, Saddles and Bridles	W. H. Carter
Notes on Elementary Equitation	Carleton S. Cooke
Cavalry Drill Regulations	United States Army
Horse Packing	Charles Johnson Post
14th Century Arabic Riding Manual	Muhammad al-Aqsarai
The Art of Travel	Francis Galton
Shanghai à Moscou	Madame de Bourboulon
Saddlebags for Suitcases	Mary Bosanquet
The Road to the Grey Pamir	Ana Louise Strong
Boot and Saddle in Africa	Thomas Lambie
To the Foot of the Rainbow	Clyde Kluckhohn
Through Five Republics on Horseback	George Ray
Journey from the Arctic	Donald Brown
Saddle and Canoe	Theodore Winthrop
The Prairie Traveler	Randolph Marcy
Reiter, Pferd und Fahrer – Volume One	Dr. C. Geuer
Reiter, Pferd und Fahrer – Volume Two	Dr. C. Geuer

The Long Riders' Guild
The world's leading source of information regarding equestrian exploration!
www.thelongridersguild.com

Lightning Source UK Ltd.
Milton Keynes UK
UKOW02f0819150914

238568UK00001B/17/P